THE LAST HOUSE ON MAIN STREET

THE LAST HOUSE ON MAIN STREET

GERTRUDE STORY

THISTLEDOWN PRESS

Canadian Cataloguing in Publication Data

Story, Gertrude, 1929-

    The last house on Main Street

    ISBN 0-920633-46-3

1. Story, Gertrude, 1929-   - Anecdotes.
2. Authors, Canadian (English) - Saskatchewan -
Anecdotes.* 3. Vanscoy (Sask.) - Biography -
Anecdotes. I. Title.

PS8587.T65Z53 1988   C813'.54   C88-098111-3
PR9199.3.S76Z47 1988

Book design by A.M. Forrie
Typeset by Apex Graphics Ltd., Saskatoon
Cover design by Robert Grey
Cover photograph by Zach Hauser

Printed and bound in Canada by
Hignell Printing Ltd., Winnipeg

Thistledown Press
668 East Place
Saskatoon, Saskatchewan
S7J 2Z5

Acknowledgements

Earlier versions of the material in this book were broadcast at various times on CBC
Regina.

This book has been published with the assistance of the Canada Council and the
Saskatchewan Arts Board.

For my mother and father—
gone on to other things,
who,
dearer now, visit me in dreams.

CONTENTS

LIVE-INS AND OCCUPATIONS

When All-that-ever-was-and-is-and-will-be snaffled Joe Story from me — by yanking him off the face of this planet (at least in any form that was of some material use to me) — when happenstance, or God, or whatever, snaffled Joe Story, *Pfft!* — just like that — out of my life, I had to learn to live, all over again.

I had to learn to do what All-there-is bids, and I found all that a very awesome (to say nothing of *tiresome*) teacher. I had to, for one thing, do an awful lot of things I didn't like, although I thought I was already doing plenty, like baking bread and hand-hoeing garden portulaca. But All-there-is gave me more to endure.

I mean, I never ever wanted to become a writer, and yet I wound up as a writer.

Things like that.

Oh, *other* people now and then wanted me to be a writer. They were mostly men; mostly teachers. And Joe Story was both a man and a teacher — and he had besides a certain kind of enthusiastic, calculated logic that was hard to turn down or turn to your own ends, unless you were a whole lot smarter than he was.

Which I wasn't.

(He had a daughter who was. And, I suspect now, a son who was but took a whole lot of trouble to hide it. But when I married the Joe Story I am talking about here, this son and this daughter were not around yet to help me to best him; so I never got in the habit of trying.)

Now, you take this business of becoming a writer. My father — to give my father credit — had the good sense not to advocate that I become a writer. (My father was not a teacher.) My father wanted me to become a teacher, but I refused. I thought I was doing enough for society if I married one, and washed his socks and cooked his dinners. And so that was that.

(My mother didn't call me Gertrude, the fighting spear maiden, for nothing.)

I have sometimes wondered since if that is why my father seemed to sign his name so swiftly, the day he had to signature the papers that signed me over—a Saskatchewan female of less than twenty-one years and therefore too vulnerable in the world not to belong to someone—to another man.

If I was not going to become a teacher, perhaps my father decided, let me be the permanent worry of one.

Who can blame a man for that?

Well, Joe Story, as it happened, was a man who supposed I could do anything he wanted me to—or at least anything that he could get me to try. And he was an extremely logical and practical man. And, yes, that *does* have something to do with this story.

Because, you see, about the seventh year that we were married we moved into another little country school teacherage. (Well, maybe it wasn't the seventh. Maybe it was the fifth or the sixth. But seven is lots more symbolic. And since I've had to become a writer, much against my own will, I like the practice of throwing in a little symbolism; I hope you don't mind.)

Anyway, as I have said, we moved into this little country teacherage and unpacked and started to live there peacefully when—*Zacko!*—this one night we found out, in a rather dramatic way, that before *we* had moved into the teacherage, a pair of skunks had moved in *under* it.

Now, to speak the full truth of it, they did not announce their presence in the characteristic way skunks have, and which is useful in making up jokes and drawing cartoons and telling real-life stories such as the one about the naked farmer who got up out of a warm bed and tiptoed out into the dark night wearing nothing but a 12 gauge Winchester. He stalked his way as a matter of course to the henhouse, for he'd wakened again to a chickeny clamour which told him "that damn skunk is back again and he's after the *third* set of chickens!"

You know as well as I do what happened. He saw the skunk. He raised and cocked the gun. The family dog came up behind him where he stood in the open door of the henhouse, and with a cold wet nose he investigated his master's naked rear fender.

The gun went off, killing not only the skunk (which made the henhouse unliveable for a year thereafter), but also 27 roosting new hens, just ready to start laying.

The skunks under King George School teacherage were more subtle than that, at first. They announced we were sharing a sort of duplex with them by indulging in the fiercest and most sharp-pitched screams I have ever heard in my protected life at two o'clock of a peaceful rural Saskatchewan morning.

This was, you see, before the mania of horror movies on the late night show. (It may have even been before the mania of television; I forget now if we then had one.)

Anyway, the skunks screamed, right under the floorboards of our bed, right in the middle of a dream I was having about a war I'd fought in once in a former life. (I was a pope of sorts, it seemed, and had just given a medal to a man who had invented a rack of some kind upon which I told him I meant to hang my washing. Have it hung, I suppose. I don't suppose even Unitarian Church ministers, in *my* dreams, ever did their own washing.)

It was a very dark night when the skunks first screamed under the floor boards of our teacherage bedroom.

"What was that?" I said, yanked wide-eyed awake, heart beating like the heart of a man upon the rack, or like the heart inside a time bomb. "What was that?" I said again, to Joe Story.

"What was what?" Joe Story said. "What was what? *I* don't hear anything!"

A skunk/a pair of skunks/an entire army of skunks screamed again underneath the bed of our teacherage bedroom. They might have been baboons planning a late night kill in a deep dark African forest; they were certainly nothing *I* had ever heard in twenty-seven safe years in Saskatchewan.

"Oh, it's nothing but skunks," he said. "I'll just bet you it's skunks," he said. "I *thought* I saw one the other day sidling under the back steps when I went to fetch wood in after supper!"

I couldn't believe that anyone in his right mind would use the

9

words "it's nothing" in the same mouthful of words that had anything at all to do with skunks. I said so.

"Look," he said. "I'm tired and you ought to be, having washed seven sets of winter underwear today on the scrub board. If *you* want to crawl under this house to interview a pair of skunks at two o'clock in the morning, that's *your* business. But if you expect *me* to do it, that's *my* business. And I can tell you right now I am not getting out of this bed to take a flashlight and wriggle into the crawl space under this house just to say How-do to a skunk.

"Are they minding their own business down there? They are. Are they keeping their stink where it belongs? They are. So what's a little yowling? It's mating season, I tell you, and they're likely a young pair on their honeymoon; so what's the matter with that?"

And that's when the skunks let go.

In the way that makes jokes and cartoons and real-life stories.

When it really happens — when it really happens to *you,* and not to someone in somebody's story — it is not funny.

"Honeymoon?" I said. "Some honeymoon! If you ask me, I'd say it's like they've been married for over twenty years and they're getting ready for the divorce!"

The smell was completely awful.

I complained a lot about it next day. And other days.

I was good at it.

Joe Story was in his own way a very patient man (I told you, I think, that he was a school teacher), but finally he said, "Now look. Complaining never solved anything. The smell is here and *we're* here." (He hardly ever was; he seemed to spend a lot of time now in the school house.) "The smell is here and we're here and the Air Wick is here and the baking soda is set out all over the house in saucers so that you can't even get a pair of shoes out of the wardrobe without stepping in it; the windows and doors are open day and night; everything that can be done has been done. So what's the use of complaining?

"Why don't you write about it?" he said, already on one leg like a stork at the porch door to put on his toe rubbers. "Why don't you just sit down today and write about it and put in a few jokes like you used to when you wrote me all those love letters, and then we'll send it to *The Western Producer* or somebody like that—people do, you know—and maybe they'll print it. And maybe they'll even pay you for it."

Well, what can a person do against such argument? I wrote it, and sent it, and got a cheque back in the mail for twelve dollars from *The Western Producer*—and from then on there was no point in trying to argue against Joe Story's logic.

"Don't complain about it to *me*," he'd say. "Write a story about it."

And that's just exactly how I began to become a writer: against my will; against my every inclination; simply because I was not bright enough to beat Joe Story at his game of logic.

So it stands to reason that by the time he flew away from me, to other realms (as writers used to say in the days of Queen Victoria), to other dimensions where they make up Joe Story's crazy kind of undefeatable logic, I wasn't trained for being a darned thing else but a writer.

I wasn't a teacher, because years ago I hadn't listened to my father. I was done already being a mother.

There was nobody now to pay you to cook and clean and grow carrots and hoe weeds out of the garden. So you gave in to All-that-is and became a writer. And found out—surprise, surprise! —that part of it was even fun, once you got the hang of it.

That was generally the part *before* you did any writing. That was the part where you went to see people and have tea with them and listen to their stories, stories about naked farmers and well-armed skunks in henhouses. Stories about moonshiners making unorthodox use of farmyard privies. There was a guy really did that, you know, so they say, somewhere just south of the village of Vanscoy.

That's where I live now. I don't live in little country teacherages anymore; even country *teachers* no longer do that. I live in a big old house which has a big old garden all set around with big old trees, on the northernmost edge of the little village of Vanscoy.

And in the fourteen years I have been here I've had mice in the basement, and sparrows in the chimney well, and cats in the garden shed. And I even had a wild sheep once (made wild from the clatter of the Vanscoy 3rd Annual Sheep Show) who

11

charged wide-eyed onto my place and refused to leave the cool safety of the caraganas no matter how we pushed or pulled or coaxed or harangued him about putting a Missouri mule to shame for mule-headedness.

But I've never had skunks here, or even a whiff of one; and you may well suppose that I am not one jot or one tittle sorry to have lived so long here without the pleasure.

THE BEST CAMOUFLAGE IS A PRIVY

The chameleon, it is said, is the master of camouflage in the world of nature, and I'd not be the one to deny it. It's not wise to deny anything you can't personally *disprove*: that's my motto; and I haven't seen a whole lot of any kind of lizard to set about disproving what has been said about the chameleon. Lizards haven't come too often my way in all the years I have lived in central Saskatchewan.

There are no lizards of any kind in, or near, or not too far away from, the big old house where I live at the edge of this little village. Joe Story bought me this house because I said I did not want to live with him, or even live at all, if I could not have it. Perhaps that wasn't very fair of me, and I know it much surprised him, for I had never been much of an asker in the twenty years before that. It was just that to me this house was too old and too warm and too beautiful for me to let it go.

That was fourteen years ago. Fourteen, or fourteen hundred.

And back then the village did not have a municipal sewer and water system. People had wells, of varying degree of iron bacteria content, which meant you might have water that was pale lemonade yellow or you might have water that was certainly louder than circus-pink lemonade. In any case, everybody in Vanscoy always appeared to be drinking lemonade, or making tea with hot lemonade (thus supposedly saving on the lemon), or boiling potatoes in lemonade and watering their garden with more of the same.

A lot of people still owned privies when we came here to live. Some had both a privy and a private field or stationary septic tank sewer system. I mean, people were not backward in

Vanscoy in 1967 and I don't want to in any way intimate that they/we were. It was Centennial Year and lots of folks had indoor bathrooms for years before that.

The place we bought had a field sewer system, but no privy. And the first year we lived in this house the field sewer system froze up tighter than a small creek in a cold winter because there was not enough snow to insulate the underground line that led to the underground dispersal field. We hauled in straw bales and insulated that forty foot of line until the place looked like the main streets of Paris during the times of the revolutionary blockades, or the university campus in Saskatoon the day the College of Agriculture throws its hijinks. But it was too late. It took money, trust me, to defrost it.

As soon as spring came, Joe Story dug a pit under the caraganas at the north end of the garden; and then one night, quite late, he hauled in the old privy from his mother's place in the city. People had been trying to get her for years to burn it, though it was sturdy and a handy place to store garden hoes, and extra bagged garbage if you didn't want strolling dogs to play tag with it before the garbage men came.

We never used the privy in our garden. We were so afraid that we might have to, that we took great care to see that we didn't have to, if you know what I mean. We moved more straw bales onto that sewer line every September, for one thing, than a lot of folks moved into their corrals and feedyards. And, of course, every spring we moved them all off again. We had more barricades and removal of barricades going on in this yard than the French and Russians have had, together, in all the years that there have been Frenchmen and Russians and revolutions.

Well now, come to think of it, I don't suppose I should say we didn't ever use the privy. It came in pretty handy for storing such things as garden hoes, and for storing bagged garbage until the garbageman came – and for forgetting you had bagged garbage stored there in it.

For several years now that privy has been a kind of symbol to me. (When you are a writer and have taken English 101 at the age of forty-seven at the university, you tend to find a lot of symbols everywhere, as I may have told you before this.) That privy seems to me to be a symbol for good old-fashioned

Saskatchewan adaptability, innovation, and outright ounce-of-prevention Boy Scout preparedness. And it's a practical example of survival-oriented camouflage.

The truth is, you see, (please keep Joe Story's secret), you aren't really supposed to own an outdoor privy in this modern village. But the way things stand (or are stored) around here, should the mayor of Vanscoy happen to take a stroll with me, for some unimaginable reason — oh well, maybe to inspect my apple trees for apples or the strawberry patch for strawberries — and if he/she were to say, "Well now, what in the blue-eyed world is *that* for?" jerking a thumb or a chin at Joe Story's mother's old privy, I could simply say (and certainly *would*), "Why, it's to store garden hoes and hoses and bagged garbage to keep it away from the dogs taking the early morning safety patrol of the village."

And that would be that, you see. The best camouflage, sometimes, is a privy that isn't a privy. I think Joe Story might have got the idea for a privy that could be one but isn't, from a story that is told here by some of the oldtimers, of a man who was just as innovative and just as adaptable and just as good at camouflage as Joe Story. Or maybe even better.

It was in the old days, the hard times days, the days of rum runners and moonshiners and the hunters of moonshine and those who made it.

When hard times hit, some succumb; but others simply rise to the situation and overcome it. If they can't make a living growing barley and selling it, why they will make a brew of that barley — or wheat or rye or potatoes or corn or parsnips — and they will sell that, because it has a readier market.

So Mr. Hopkins did just that. (No no, of *course* his name wasn't really Mr. Hopkins. Does his name matter? I mean, he's dead now; long gone, dead and gone now. If you are interested in checking the safety and/or potency of his product I'm just afraid I can't help you on that. I mean, we do protect our own here. It's a rule, sort of, and it operates in all little towns all across this land, not just here in Vanscoy.)

But I hope you can take the storyteller's word for it: Mr. Hopkins was awfully good at his work. He was so good at it, in fact, that he was taken to task for it regularly by the Royal Saskatchewan Mounties—thirteen times a year was nothing, so it is said, for them to show an interest. So naturally he became very good at finding places to house his product; and they were creative stashes, to say the least.

Still, no matter how he hid his still those sharp-eyed, sharp-nosed Mounties found it.

By the same token, Mr. Hopkins was not a man to give up easily. Times were too tough. So the next time he built a still he didn't even consider a poplar bluff in a hidden gulley twelve miles from home, or an abandoned trapper's shack down by the river. He simply dug a deep pit at one end of his own farm-yard, and built a room in it, and covered it over with grassed sod, and with the chimney pipe of the boiler coming up inside a wigwam of fresh willow posts he had set upon the site to make it look as though they were there curing.

From the dug pit room he carved a tunnel to the edge of the shelterbelt nearer the house. And there he built a brand-new privy with the joke book half-moon window. (Maybe Mr. Hopkins was pretty good at jokes and symbolism and that's why he opted for a half-moon window; I am sorry that I will never know.) And Mr. Hopkins went into that outhouse sometimes fourteen times a day, in busy season—and it had nothing to do with eating fresh rhubarb for breakfast either, though he may have told a body or two that, if they were the kind of folks it was best to tell it to. Mr. Hopkins made many trips to his outhouse because he was a most particular brewmaster who cooked a careful (and pleasant) brew.

And whenever he reversed his tracks and came up the tunnel from the brew pit to the entrance, Mr. Hopkins made it a habit to check through the half-moon window in the privy door before he stepped out.

If someone had driven in since he'd gone down to check on the cooking, Mr.Hopkins would slip his suspenders off his shoulders and undo the top button of his dirt-colored pants. Then he would step out the door, hoisting his galluses up with a shrug of the shoulders, meanwhile doing up the top button on his pants.

"Anything I can do for you boys?" he would call. (Although sometimes he had to call "you ladies" instead. Women got pretty

16

liberated out here on the Saskatchewan prairies. At least they did around Vanscoy. And sometimes they drove around in their horse buggies or Model T coupes calling on people like Mr. Hopkins to collect signatures for the vote.)

And if he decided to his own satisfaction the callers were bona fide callers and not overt or undercover Mounties (or the devil's own sons – informers) he would relax, and stuff both hands in his pockets, and teeter back and forth on his heels – heel, toe; heel, toe. And he would say, "Now, I betcha if you was to turn right at the gate there when you leave here, and if you was to go due south to the next road allowance and keep watch for the last fence post but one, and if that fence post happens to have a patcha buck brush around it, and if you was to feel around there in about the middle of that patch, you just might find something interesting there, supposin you're out today collectin field sparra eggs."

Then he would take one hand out of one pocket and shake hands with the sparrow egg collector, and then he would put his hand back in his pocket again, and you just might hear something there inside crinkle a little as he called good-bye to the departing coupe or buggy. It was said Mr. Hopkins could tell the difference between a two or a five just by feel. And he never ever bothered to saddle a horse and race off after anyone who had underpaid him; he just didn't have anything of interest to report to that person the next time he came, on the subject of field sparrow eggs.

He was very good on faces, was Mr. Hopkins, so it is said.

The story grows with the telling, I'm sure. Isn't that the way of stories? The way of storytellers? If we were content to tell only the plain, uninteresting, unvarnished, this-world truth about things, we would all know for sure today whether there had ever really been an ark large enough to hold two of every earth species, plus their feed and water, plus a pit privy large enough to hold all that forty days' worth of manure.

We're great ones for camouflage, we earthlings, I sometimes think; even those of us who have the adaptability and courage to people Saskatchewan and the little prairie towns in it, like Vanscoy.

THE PSYCHOLOGY OF SPARROW SPRINGS

When it is springtime, you always know it by the sparrows.
It may be dark and cloudy and dreary, and a darned metric
metre of snow might have just fallen—but if it is springtime,
you will know it by the sparrows; and mostly you will be glad.

You will know it by the sparrows' song. Sparrows sing—I don't
know: softer? more cheerful, more hopeful? more
melodious?—in a way you can tell is different, when once again
it is spring. At least when it is spring in the country, or spring
in a little village; for those are the only springs I know about,
and they seem to suit me pretty well.

Well, the one part of a sparrow-foretold spring suits. I am not
so sure about the other. For there are two ways, at least in the
house where I live, that you can tell spring by the sparrows.

Sparrows always seem to make their way into your chimney
well here, and flutter and flit and scrape their toenails against
the sheet metal there, and scare you to death—not because
you believe it's a ghost, as you once did, briefly, when Joe Story
had flown this earth and your searching mind was engaged in
impressing you with a hard and calculated kind of teaching, but
because you are afraid you know what it would feel like to be
trapped.

So when you hear the desperate flutterings inside your metal
chimney well, you know you will have to leave everything
else—spring gardens to be ploughed or even poems to be
written—and retrieve that lousy little sparrow before he/she
breaks your heart.

As the first one did. The one you found, too late, when you
and not Joe Story had the job of cleaning your chimney.

I don't know how they get in there. The sparrows. At first I thought they likely sat on the edge of the chimney face to warm their toes and their tails—Who can blame them?—and that they fell in when the carbon dioxide (or the carbon monoxide or the whatever-it-is that seduces the one hovering over the fumes) seduced them, *plonk-surprise!* into the long hollow well of the chimney.

But after there was only me to do things I wanted done but was too unhandy or squeamish or scared spitless to do myself, I climbed clenched-toothed to the top of this tall two-storey house and measured the chimney top and then climbed down the same way and had a grating made for the chimney, smiling. I almost flew back up the ladder then; I almost floated across the ridgepole like Mary Poppins, I so believed that would be the last time I would have to scoop sparrows alive or, worse, alive no longer, out of the chimney clean-out in my basement.

Last spring there were ghostly flutterings again in my chimney. I cussed Saskatchewan winds and snow and ice, for I firmly believed a combination of all three must have somehow shifted the grate awry on that chimney. But by then I knew that cussing would not solve anything. Hadn't I heartily tried to get by on it for some several years now? (And to no avail, as the old catechism was fond of saying when it wanted to chastise you for exercising the will it said God gave you.)

So anyway, I hauled out that thirty-foot, three hundred dollar, aluminum extension ladder with the rope and the rollers built in; the one a child or even a middle-aged Saskatchewan woman was supposed to be able to raise, like Lazarus from the dead, only more useful to you. That ladder raising always works, if you are mad enough at something.

Or really, really desperate.

Anyway, I went up on the roof and checked the grating and it was solid as river rock up there, and sitting four-square to boot.

I couldn't figure it out. But the active, ever-helpful (and very dumb!) creative right-hand side of the brain comforted me with the scenario that the wind had lifted that metal grating just as a sparrow had flown by, minding his/her own housebuilding business, and the grating had whapped her (it was a her by

19

now), like a ping-pong paddle whaps a ping-pong ball or a bad-minton racquet whaps a birdie, just where it's supposed to go.

Yes, I *know* the scenario was stupid. But there's no accounting for one's right-hand brain and there's simply no assurance that it came along with the left-hand side when you finally went to college. And if I am telling this just the way it happened (and I am) then I can't be expected to leave out the part about my creative but rather dim-witted right brain. It so often makes me appear to be stupid. But then, if the shoe fits, perhaps the writer-philosopher better wear it; maybe both are in need of a little humility, and anyway, the shoe that wears softest is the sin you have openly confessed.

Since I have sunk here to the level of philosophizing, instead of getting on with the sparrow's story, I might as well confess that I was born an incurable optimist. I always expect that the least little thing I do to help myself will snaffle me out of any pickle I get into. I'm the kind who expects a flat tire to inflate again if I will only have the good grace to get out of the car and look at it. Sometimes, when looking has done nothing, I will say, "Oh my, too bad; too bad, old dear!" and then tap it gently with the toe of one boot in sympathy. The tire never, never re-inflates on its own, but I earnestly expect the next one to do so.

And so it was with the sparrows. I issued a mind memo to all and sundry in the vicinity of the village of Vanscoy not to fly past my chimney in a high wind on housebuilding or on any other kind of a project lest the metal grating rise on its hind legs and whap them, badminton racquet-like, into ghostly oblivion inside my chimney.

But this spring there was another one.

I was working on a really important piece of work. (Important to me and to the village office where a careful account is kept of those who do not pay their sewer and water bills.) It was a book manuscript and books do not really make you any money, but they do tend to bring in some sewer and water bill funds by somehow making people want to pay that rather crazy woman to come and talk to them in the small towns where they live. So you see what I mean by this work I was doing being important. But it was making me feel really mean because it

was at the typing stage and typing always makes me feel so
. . . well, so mean and awful.

That is because I do not type one whit better today than I
did when I was first teaching myself to type, well over thirty
years ago, on a scrawny little manual Upthedyke (or Upthe-
creek, or Upthesomething) with six missing keys. I was
teaching myself to type then because Joe Story had said it would
be such a great help. I didn't mind, did I? Why, my goodness,
when the school exams were written out in his own hand
sometimes the little ones had some trouble reading the questions, and I knew what the little ones were like sometimes —
they might be too shy to ask Teacher and then their grades
would go down and that would be awful, now wouldn't it?

Well, when you are young and gullible you believe the darndest things, now don't you? It's a pity, sometimes, the things
that you will believe.

But all right now, I was saying that I really felt mean this
particular spring day, and I was so pressed for time and that
just made me feel meaner. And so I said to the sparrow fluttering fitfully in my metal chimney, "Well, you can just darn well
stay there, you dummy; that'll teach you; and there are oodles
more sparrows to sing soft melodies when it is spring."

But of course, some other mind would not let me do that.
I don't know where this other mind comes from. Certainly not
from the super-dim right-hand side of my brain. But this other,
ever-hopeful, better mind just suddenly appeared and I knew
I would not be allowed to let it go at that.

"Just go right down and get her out," it said. "It will only take
a minute."

"Hah!" I said to this other mind. "And where were you last
spring? And the spring before? And the spring even before that?
Hah! and Hah! again!"

"Take only a minute", indeed. As if I didn't know better.
Everytime it happens it takes all morning to get out a sparrow. I have to find a cardboard box of just the right size to fit
over the clean-out hole, and find a flashlight that lights and will
make the sparrow think the dark cardboard box is really
sunlight and therefore freedom. I have to find a board to slip

between the chimney wall and the cardboard box once the sparrow has been successfully decoyed.

And when all is in place you can often sit an hour before he/she will have the courage to follow through. And if you do not sit like Buddha or a silent river rock the whole time you'll be sitting more like two hours.

Still, "Trust me," said the other mind this time. "This time trust me, trust me. She'll be out in no time; she's a quick one, this one."

Well, I went. I found the box for the trap, and I found the flashlight, and I took the plywood bake board to slip over the box trap should she choose to fly into it. I got everything laid ready to hand. I began to open the clean-out door.

"Be quick with the trap there!" the other mind said.

"Naw," I said. "What's the all-fired . . . *Oops!*" I said.

For the sparrow was out and gone, just like that.

And where was she? Why, where except upstairs in my kitchen, where I'd just been laying out a hurried breakfast of brown bread and strawberry jam when my other mind made me a savior to a misguided middle-aged sparrow.

I may be wrong about her age though; for she shot out of the clean-out hole quicker than I'd ever gone up a ladder, even the time I thought I was Mary Poppins off to the roof tops to solve my sparrow worries for a lifetime with a piece of bend-ed grate.

My, she was quick! But now where was I with a sparrow making nervous passes over my late breakfast, and me without an extra crust of bread in the house?

None of that fazed the other mind, though. "Don't worry, now," said mind. "Follow me. Go with the flow, my dear, and it will all be over in a trice."

Here's the truth of it: I have learned, in the past few years of living more or less like a hermit, that when that other mind calls me "my dear" and says things like "in a trice", why, I am better off to trust it. I myself, you might as well know it, have never called myself "my dear" even once in over fifty years and am not likely to start to do it. So when it happens, I know the speaker is not me or even my dumb right-hand brain, and so I might just as well trust it.

"Up the stairs," said mind. I upped it.

Wh-wh-UPP! That was sparrow, whizzing from my bread and jam to the kitchen window.

"Trap her with those pretties now," said mind. I drew the window drapes. Sparrow fluttered into silence.

"Now up the stairs for a large dark sheet," said mind.

"A sheet?" said I.

"Well well well; just first open the outside door then," said this calmly calculating mind which now seemed to own me. "And put on warm things; heavy things; outdoor things; and spectacles for the eyes; you are such a timid one, my dear, I would have you better girded."

It all seemed stupid, but I did it. And then I got a picture flash, there . . . somewhere . . . inside or just outside the head . . . to show me the why of the sheet. So I charged upstairs to the linen closet and then charged back down again with a queen-size sheet and pinned it, one corner, to the kitchen drapes where Sparrow began her fluttering all over again as soon as ever she felt it; and I fetched a nail and hammer and tacked the other corner to the kitchen door, up above the flashing where the nail mark won't show. And there, *Presto,* mind and I had made a lighted alley-way for an escape route for Madam Sparrow, as sure as the buffalo hunters once made pound trap routes, not for the escape but for the capture of the things they hunted; trap routes which they trusted, so long as they could just get the buffalo started off in the right direction. A buffalo pound trap route was the quickest way to the dinner table in those days.

I did not want to eat this sparrow, of course. I just wanted to get shut of her. I grabbed for the drapes to release her into the trap.

"Not *this* side the pretties!" mind said, mind very nearly snapped. "Slide an arm gently through and draw open the other. Then she'll be heading the direction we want her, and she'll simply arrow out."

I did.

Ph-ph-phl-phlt!

That's all there was to it.

23

Then, because I had all those outdoor clothes on, I followed Sparrow out, shutting the door securely, you might well suppose, behind me. And though I did not want to, mind made me step towards the garden far enough so that I could see the offending chimney.

I was standing just right. The sun was just right. The shadows were just right. I noticed a small opening, hardly mouse-size, in the cement skirting atop the brick-work in that chimney. A sparrow might consider to build her nest safely there, since the grackles have made sparrow lives so unbearable in the garden pines.

An opening hardly large enough to fit a mouse.

"Oh for pete's sake," I said, thinking of mixing patching cement; thinking of my book, and no breakfast, and the size of that darn aluminum ladder.

"There, there; we'll leave it for a day or two," said mind. "Then one of these fine mornings I shall arrange for you to bump your head or stub your toe or to get two rejections in the same mail. You will soon be up the ladder and we shall mend it all then."

I don't mind saying it's a luxury and a comfort to belong to a mind like that if you are a little woman, an impatient woman, a middle-aged and a middling stupid woman, living in a big old holey house alone, in a sparrow-ridden (though otherwise lovely) large old house at the edge of a little village on the prairies.

STEALING THE SOUL WITH A BLACK BOX CAMERA

When I was a kid and going to a country school about the size of somebody's hat-box, we put on a play once wherein a mean little, spoiled little girl did nothing much but beller, "I don't wanna get my picture took, so there!"

Well, I'm a little like that spoiled little girl. I cannot bear to get *my* picture took, and that is that. It's awful, to be over fifty and still have to admit you cannot handle that. Yet it's worse, somehow, to try to pretend that you can.

I've always hated it. There's not too much in this world I have hated in my time, but that is one: getting my soul stolen by a wicked black box camera. And I have always avoided it, as best I could — even offering to be the one to snap the shutter so that others can get their pictures taken; even offering to do this after I grew a firm reputation for cutting off everybody's heads when I was the one to do the snapping.

When the pictures came back short-headed, I used to pencil in hair and hats and bald spots — and even whole faces, if I had to — on the people I'd beheaded, back in the days when the printers left white margins on your snapshots just so you could do that. And then I would put those pictures in photo albums, or send them to the cousins or uncles or whoever had had their heads cut off by me. And I got pretty good at pencilling in hair and bald spots, but I never got any better at taking pictures.

I kept on doing it, though. So I wouldn't have to get my own picture taken. I suppose I'd have been keener on taking a chance if I'd known the picture-taker was as good at beheading people as I was. In this day and age everyone else I know throws away the ones that have no heads on. But this happens to be a time when most people are good at whatever they do, so you can never really count on anybody else cutting your head off and so circulating a copy of your living soul no farther than the waste basket or the garbage bin.

Sometimes I think about the odd ways I have, and I have thought about this one quite a lot lately. I think maybe I have caught the reason for it; the reason I cannot bear to have my picture taken. Actually, if I'm going to admit to things, I guess I'd better say I think I know *two* reasons why.

Number one has to do with being plain as plain, and having just far too many wrinkles.

If you cannot see the wrinkles — that is, if you do not look in mirrors or at photographs — there is nothing to stop you from being eighteen or eight or even three, if you want to, for a day or for a year or two. But you simply cannot be those things if you own a lot of mirrors or any number of recent photographs.

I haven't had wrinkles all my life, of course. At least I don't think I have. If you hardly ever look in a mirror that is a hard thing to remember. But likely, I haven't. So I have to tell you the number two reason I cannot bear to stand determined or posed or openly squinting in front of anybody's camera.

When I was young I had antisocial feet.

Of course, there's more to it than that. I just want you to get used to the idea of a grandmotherly sort of woman talking about sweaty feet before I go any further. Because I suppose now I have to tell you the obvious next step: the result of that.

If I don't, I suppose I'll get by by saying that of course my mother had to find a way around that, when baking soda would not work and I refused to change my socks three times a day in summer. Besides, my mother didn't want to scrub twenty-one pairs of socks every week on the scrub board. Who can blame her? Goodness knows, she had washing enough and to spare with five other Dirty Thirties farm children, even if the rest had feet as dry as the farm fields and as sweet as the pasture roses which, like my mother's children, grew and flourished whether or not there was so much as a drop of rain all summer.

But my mother was a thinker. It didn't take her long to figure out that running shoes were the worst thing in the world for making the feet nervous, hot summers. Only thing was, running shoes were also the cheapest way to shoe six pairs of farm child feet. (My mother was not a one to permit her children to run about barefoot; bare feet in her book had no class; they had not one single thing to recommend them.)

So my mother kept on thinking until she hit upon the principle of air conditioning: she simply cut five jagged holes in the tops of my new running shoes, right over the toes, until they looked a little like Julius Caesar's Roman sandals.

Ugly as sin.

I was so ashamed of those running shoes with the holes in them that I would rather have died than wake up in the morning and know I'd have to put them on again. I prayed for the Lord Jesu my soul to take night after night, but (of course) he never did; He likely had enough sandals of his own, and besides, He was also pretty busy too, likely, writing new catechism verses for me to learn hot Sundays, and in German.

Naturally, I never told my mother I could not bear to wear holey running shoes. You did not do that in those days; you just died every day, and wore them.

One day that summer one of our stylish aunts came over with her new box camera. She'd been working for quite a while by then in town in a restaurant or a meat market—I forget now which—and she had plenty of money for things like new cloche hats, and fringed and beaded dance dresses, and new box cameras.

And of course she wanted to take a picture of us children. She said we were too cute for words and so she had better put us in a picture. And though I tried to run away she ran me down and then lined us up under the maple trees against the sun and told us to say *Plea-ea-ease,* while she checked and adjusted and checked again the new box camera and said things like, "Just a little minute more, now!" over and over again.

When the pictures were printed my face was so screwed up with pain of two sorts that I heard two visiting cousins tell each other whilst consulting the photo album, "Oh, my now, doesn't the little one just take after her mother's grandma like a face in a basin of clear wash water?"

My mother's grandmother, I'd have you to know, was plain and pale and wispy and very full of wrinkles.

I told all that the other day to the photographer who came to my house here in the little village where I live, to take my picture. I did not ask him to. I did not want him to. A publisher sent him.

He was very nice. He told funny stories about *his* mother's grandmother and pretended he was not stealing my soul at all with his version of my aunt's black box camera while he bade me sit at the big dining room table where I often write, nights, by the light of a coal oil lamp because that is easier on the eyes when you are over fifty and bifocaled.

The sun had not even set, but we lit the coal oil lamp so that the flame would show up in the pictures.

The cameraman looked in some ways somewhat like a Lutheran pastor I had once, one of the very kindly ones. Just the same, I felt like a little girl again, standing on her toes in the too-short grass to hide the holes in her running shoes. I haven't seen those printed pictures yet, but I just bet you anything you want to bet that camera will forget I was really only five that day, and it will give me wrinkles
wrinkles
wrinkles.

As if to steal your soul was not bad enough, it will remind me what happens to bodies, whether or not you keep track of them in a mirror.

I could almost wish that beautiful, bearded young man had not bothered to come here, to my big old house, where I can be five years old any day of the week that I want to so long as I am alone; here on the edge of a little village on the wide Saskatchewan prairie.

GOING FOR THE MAIL (AND WHAT YOU GET)

Whenever I go for the mail, in the little town where I live, I am reminded of two little jokes. One of them is on me, and one of them is on those of us who live in little towns, in little (or even big) villages. We seem to have a lot of little jokes, those of us who live in small prairie towns. They get to be like in-jokes: they are funny to the people who live in small towns, but not, much, to anyone else.

Maybe, like the in-jokes at family reunions or at office parties, they serve a purpose of sorts: maybe they help us to keep together; to work together and to live together. In a little place, where people live close together and yet are as different from each other as night is from day and the sunlight, it's maybe pretty important to have a few small jokes everyone agrees are at least "kinda" funny.

Like, we used to have our little joke about Mr. Gilbertson all those years he sat on the village council. We told him about it, too, of course. We used to say that Mr. Gilbertson was so darn neat he went around town, nights, secretly with a flashlight, picking up stray straws in the streets so that the town would be neat enough so that he would not be ashamed to be sitting on its council.

Some even used to say that Mr. Gilbertson carried a spare pocket comb, to curry the grass in front yards here and there as he went about town, if the grass in those yards wasn't quite tidy enough to suit him.

Those were the jokes about Mr. Gilbertson. But the truth of things was that Mr. Gilbertson—and Mr. Vermeulen and Mr. Snow and Mr. Abel, and a few other Misters who have sat, over the years, on this little village's council — rarely sat. They were too busy. Oh, they sat every Tuesday night for a while; sat in a little closed-in room with the smoke so thick it would have cured a batch of fresh herring before the meeting was over; sat to plan how to look after this village on an assessment roll and a mill rate so low anybody nowadays would wonder why the place didn't go under in ten years' time instead of becoming a prime place for even city folks to live and to commute from.

Part of the reason is because those early councillors not only planned what work had to be done in order to keep the place running on a pittance, they actually did the work, and at no pay save the councillor's stipend. (If ever a reward was more aptly named than "stipend", I have yet to hear about it.)

Those councillors graded the streets (and repaired and cussed and cajoled the grader before and after they had done the grading). They cleaned the village well when it needed cleaning. They scrounged pumps for the spring flooding from their own bosses or businesses and manned them, day and night, if need be. They helped to build the sewer and the water systems when the time came. And when that awful alarm bell rang at the sewer lift station, they climbed into overalls and waders and gas masks and went below themselves to repair what needed repairing, because that was quicker and cheaper. And most of the people in town never even knew somebody had thrown too many Pampers down the toilet again, unless they'd been outside and heard the ringing of that sewer alarm bell.

Or else they heard about it when they went for the mail next morning, to the post office.

Which brings me to the first little joke I often think about when *I* am going for the mail, most mornings, to the Vanscoy post office. The joke is, that in a little town folks don't bother to buy a daily paper; they go for the news to the post office. It's true. If you want to know who has had a baby or who has won an election (or who has lost one), if it's between newscasts on your radio, and your TV and phone are on the fritz, not to worry; just hie you to your local small town post office.

It's a terrific way to get your news of a morning (except you have to answer remarks about the weather five or six times for each new person who comes into the lobby). I think everybody in Vanscoy likes it.

In fact, I know one couple who had their own little in-joke within this larger village in-joke. Both of them were fond of the morning visit, but a woman has more morning duties than a retired farmer so this neighbour used to say, "Walter always beats me in the morning getting away to fetch the mail, so I have to get all the news secondhand when he gets back, and you have to wonder, sometimes, if he hasn't missed something!"

In my case, I live right across the road from the school, but when I want to know what's going on at that school, I always go to the post office.

If there's to be a wedding or a fowl supper; if somebody hardly over the age of 35 has just become a new grandmother; if dog licences are due again (or if you've been visited by somebody's dog, licenced or unlicenced, by surprise in your own back garden); if there's to be a ball tournament, or a snowmobile rally a few towns down the road: you will read it on a wall poster or you will hear about it at the post office.

People who used to live in small towns but don't any longer say they miss this sort of thing, and I can understand that. We Storys lived for nearly a year in a big city once and all I ever heard from the mailman was that there was seven cents due on another letter, or that the dog had bitten him again. (Until the year we lived in Calgary I always thought dogs only bit mailmen in cartoons, or in stories that never seemed funny to me. I always wanted the mailman to have bitten the dog instead.)

I live a rather insular sort of life. It often doesn't sound like it, and people who have been trying to get me on the phone for three days handrunning, without success, simply won't believe it. But I really do. I work at home, and so that is my protection. I mean to say, if you are in the habit of going into the worlds inside your mind at seven o'clock of a morning so you can put that world and the people in it down on paper, you need that kind of aloneness.

It would not do, of course, to begin to prefer those inner worlds to the exclusion of this, more solid, planet. Yet there are days I would not see a single living soul or hear a human

31

voice except my own. (Except my own, when I've been happily surprised by the honey song of a tiny wren, the sound gushing in with the spring sun through an open window so clear and eventful I say "Oh!", aloud, like that, because I cannot help it. Except my own, when I've tripped for the third time that day over my own shoe laces and just escaped taking a short-cut down the stairs because of it, and so I say "Oh!"– or maybe other things – again.)

But when you are one who works at home, and when you are working well, you sometimes write all day and so you walk out under the night-time stars to get your mail out of the box in the lobby of the post office.

But if you have spent the best part of a week like that, it's no good, you decide. If your only contact with homo sapiens is going to be somebody not sapiens enough to quit tripping over her own shoe laces, it is just simply high time to go for the mail in the bright light of morning day; and, in fact, rather early.

That's when you see the action. That's when you get to say "Hello there!" every few steps, some days. There are a lot of retired folks living in this town and they are of the generation that believes in getting up early.

So if it's early spring, let's say, and there's been a surprise fall of snow overnight – this being, after all, Saskatchewan – you might meet four people on the same mission: they're calling for their mail on the way to sweep the snow off the walk at Gramma Vermeulen's. (Until we came to live in Vanscoy, I never used to believe there'd be a woman in a small town anywhere that *everybody* would call Gramma, unless that town was in a horse opera or sit-com on Yankee-style television.) And you yourself already know, because you pass her place on your way for the mail, when those would-be snow shovellers get there they're going to find that Gramma is already up and has already swept it.

There's this about Gramma Vermeulen: she doesn't go out and sweep her own walk so early because she is Dutch and remembers scrubbing the stone front steps of houses there with a scrub stone; she does it because she is neat – and because she is so almighty feisty.

A few years ago she was, it is said, on her way to a permanent stay in a wheel chair. But she told her pain she would have none of it, and now, well past the years the old Bible text allots to us earthlings, she goes out and sweeps her own walk every snowy morning.

But when people say they are on their way to do it for her, you say nothing. You know part of the trip is to say "Hello, how are you?" to her. It's called "touching", I hear, today, by some psychologists. Whatever it's called, I don't want to tamper with what works.

If you're early enough you're going to catch the little kids, running late because they talked their mothers into letting them take their bikes to school (so that they could go quicker!). Some are new in town, and so they're not sure if they're supposed to answer your "Hello there!" or not. In the city, sometimes, they've been trained not to do that. It doesn't seem to take them long to learn it's OK, here in the little village of Vanscoy.

I said when I first started this . . . well, this *talk,* I guess I might as well say (It *sounds* like talk to me inside my head, when I am putting it down on the paper). . . . Anyway, I said earlier on that there are two jokes I often think of when I go for the mail – early enough to see bright, shy little kids or as late as I please, because the Vanscoy post office has a lobby that is almost 100 per cent always open.

I've told you the one about the post office being better than a newspaper. The second one has to do with me, and with my deficiencies.

The house where I live lies but two blocks due north (or at least in a straight line, whatever the direction) of the Vanscoy post office. The first week we lived here, when there happened to be no one but me around one day to go for the mail, I got lost going to the post office. I was so embarrassed it took me years to get over it.

Then I discovered the principle of exaggeration. Sinners use it, I've heard, to have a heck of a good time the week before they go to Confession. (I think then it is called the Might As Well Be Hanged For A Sheep As A Goat principle.) Anyway, I somehow discovered, if you have a weakness, a sin, a shortcoming, a failing – if, in plain words, you have been short-changed by All-there-ever-was-and-is-and-will-be in the matter of an in-built directional compass — it is best to advertise it, rather than to hide it.

"Your sins will out" is an old saying that holds true, so when I am on my way home again, the mail under one arm, and someone calls from across the street, "You didn't get lost again, I see!" I simply smile and call back, "I'm carrying young Joseph's Boy Scout compass."

As you can see, you sometimes get all you need and more, when you go for the mail in broad daylight, leaving your inner worlds behind in a large old house on the northernmost end of your village's short Main Street.

GETTING LOST, AND GETTING LOST, AND GETTING LOST

I think I have told you before that I was born without a compass inside my head; that I can get lost in my own house, almost, going from one room to another, unless I carry a ball of thread, like Theseus on his way to interview the man-eating Minotaur in his marvelously mazed den, so I can wind myself back where I started.

I am forever getting lost, and it saddens me, and I resent it. I mean, it is still a puzzle to me, after all these years of wondering about it, why I should come from a family that could find their separate and individual ways back to the homestead through blinding snow storms in the dead of a prairie winter, and yet here am I, born totally bereft of any navigational genes whatsoever. And so I get lost so often.

The worst thing is, you see, that not only do I get lost a lot, but I never believe I am going to. To compensate me for having been born with no compass to speak of inside my head, The Big Joker, The Giver of All Things, gave me when I was born this terrible optimism about everything.

Awful things happen to me every day of the week, and I just don't believe them. I call them "blessings in disguise" and try to wiggle out of them somehow, and then forget them. So every time I get back home again after having been lost in a little dinky toy automobile in some uncharted and rock-infested gulley or pasture in the wilds of Saskatchewan, I just seem to pretend it never ever happened.

And I am always sure it will never happen again.

The reason I keep getting lost is two-fold: Number 1, I can't read maps very well, although I own about five thousand of them; and Number 2, I want to see as much of Saskatchewan as I can before I die, so that I will know where I want to go again when I am only spirit.

Now, as you very well know, you can't see too much of *any* place by sticking to the main paved highways, or by travelling the same country roads over and over and over. So, if I happen to be going down to Central Butte, let's say; four Thursdays in a row, let's say (as I happened to do not so awfully long ago, and which is therefore why I even remember it), I don't want to get lost, now, do I, when I do it? I mean, I'm going on business. So if I happen to know that Central Butte lies more south of Vanscoy than it lies north or east or west of it (because even *I* can't read a map badly enough not to see that), why, what is more sensible than to go south, south, south, on any good road you can, once you get out of Vanscoy?

Well, nothing; if the Giver of All Things hadn't put a river between Central Butte and Vanscoy! You have got to *cross* that darn river, I have just lately found out; and so you had better hit the Riverhurst Ferry, or the Gardiner Dam, or Outlook town, or even Saskatoon city, on the paved roads that take you there, before you start southing like Henry Kelsey on his way to chart new lands for the king.

Now, *here's* a surprise for you. Maybe. This story is *not* about getting lost, although the title and I have just said so. It is really about not looking a gift horse in the mouth. It is, in fact, about knowing a gift when the Giver of All Things throws one in your face to catch your attention.

The last time I went to Central Butte I was a little short of time already, so I could not resist looking for a short-cut. That was my excuse, you see. It is always legitimate to try out a new strange road if you are short of time and so have to be looking for a short-cut. And lo and behold, of course there presented itself a lovely high gravel road to the south. And I just *knew* it would take me directly into Central Butte if I would only take it.

But Good Sense, drumming somewhere there deep inside the euphoria of self-confidence, pleaded with me to at least for goodness sake check it out on the map first. I could never stand travelling with a whiner. So I got out my faithful ten-year-old map of Saskatchewan. I unfolded the map, promising it more sticky tape for the torn parts once I got it home again, and I peered at it. When you have to wear bifocals and you do not like or want them, it seems you have to hold everything within two inches of your eyeballs or else you are forever reading Saskatoon as VaSoon, or something like that, just because it sits, on your map, next to Vanscoy.

I had just about got to the cussing stage—the stage you reach just before you figure everything out (or believe you have)—when a car pulled up beside me. I heard it. It always happens. People are all very courteously curious all over Saskatchewan. I knew somebody meant to say, "Are you lost?" Every time I am sitting in my little car with my head lost in a map, half of Saskatchewan seems to want to drive up and say it. I wasn't. And so I didn't want to hear it.

I kept my nose and eyes wrapped in the map. Good Sense tried to tell me something. I refused to listen.

Then *zap!*, the Giver of All Things tore right through the faint murmur Good Sense was making. And It bellered into my brain: DISCOURTESY WILL NOT BE TOLERATED! YOU MOVE YOUR BIG FAT MAP OUT OF THIS CAR AND TALK!

I moved it.

"Are you lost?" said the driver.

I said that oh no indeed, I wasn't. But the driver told me anyway, the good gravel road I meant to take would peter out into corduroyed coulees and blind ends, and the only way to get to Central Butte at *all* from where we were, was to go *east*, of all things; and *then* south; and only then, when you had back-tracked the same miles west as you went east out of your way in the first place, would you get to Central Butte. But then, what could I expect, the driver said, wasn't this Saskatchewan?

Needless to say, I thanked the driver heartily; after all, I, too, was born in courteous Saskatchewan. And it turned out to be exactly so, so I was doubly grateful when I got where I was going and found out I might just as well be sitting just then in four foot of ravine water where the road had given away over night to a sharp drop you had better know about if you didn't want to cool your Toyota's heels in fresh spring water.

I was grateful to the driver who had steered me right. But I was so miffed with the Giver of All Things for interfering, I couldn't be civil to Him/Her/It again for a week, after I got back home to the welcoming cocoon walls of my house on Vanscoy's well-charted Main Street.

STEPPING LIVELY

I'm a good walker. I know there is no point in bragging about that to anybody in Saskatchewan, where the roads are long and the miles are sometimes endless, but I am a good walker, all the same.

It used to be that I had to be. When I was young. My father did not keep horses suitable for riding, and machines and I did not get along. I don't know why that is. It is a mystery to me why some people can operate anything with wheels or tracks or wings or gliders, but some people have to get by on two somewhat flat feet.

I've never been any different, either. The only time I tried to ride a bicycle when I was young, I had to jump off it going down hill at maybe sixty miles-the-hour, because the cows I was herding had taken off *up* the same hill, but towards the neighbour's green oats, as soon as they saw me warping and weaving atop those two narrow wheels.

I never tried a bicycle again.

Joe Story, when I met him about ten years after that, was a man crazy about motorcycles, and he used to take me and his dog for crazy rides in the sandhills. But he scared me spitless the day he zipped us all through the air off a promontory in somebody's pasture and the dog flew over my head and landed feet first in an ant hill. (At least *he* got a quick start to the getaway when those red ants began to see redder over the intrusion.) For my part, I would never ride on that motorcycle again, although Joe Story coaxed and (foolish man!) even dared me. The dog did, though.

I never learned to drive a car, until there was no Joe Story to take me wherever I needed to go. If there was some place I *wanted* to go, it was often a pleasure to walk. It still is, and I still do it. I like walking, although I own a neat little silver Japanese eaglet which swoops me safely from one end of Saskatchewan almost to the other, even on icy roads, in the heart of a Saskatchewan winter; even on icier roads, when the weather man has lied to you that it is spring.

I like walking, although it takes time to walk. Time, on Planet Earth these days, is at an all-time premium, and even I know what it sometimes costs you to walk. I like walking because all you have to take along to have a good time is a silver speculating mind — and maybe, if it's hot and summertime, an umbrella.

I used to program the day to try to make time to go walking. But now, I've discovered, it's a lot wiser to walk all day if you have to, in order to give the mind time enough to program just exactly what *it* wants you to do. I found that out quite by chance, this past winter, because I spent some money I felt awfully guilty about.

I used to walk, winters, now and again on these old wooden skis, see? On Joe Story's old, mended, fur-trapping skis, the ones he wore winter weekends when he stopped being a teacher for two days and became a fur trapper instead. But my heels kept slipping off those skis and upsetting me. And even if they stayed on, I always made tracks like a pigeon-toed prairie chicken crossing the fields on two staves off an old wooden barrel.

So when the new waxless skis came on the market I went to town and bought a pair; just like that. But, naturally, as soon as I brought them home some old thrift pattern in my mind reared its ugly head and said, "Tut, tut; what a waste of money!"

Well, I've learned how to handle that. (It's not the first time I've heard that scolder.) To make sure the money *wasn't* wasted, I began to go out on those brazen red plastic skis every day, no matter what the temperature, even in brazen Celsius.

And my mind told me to concentrate on the toes of those skis for a while until I got the hang of it, on the track, and on the rhythm, and on nothing else. I'd heard about emptying the mind and even tried all one winter to do it, but I never really believed it could happen; I always thought it was some kind of crazy East Asian joke on the Western world, until I hypnotized myself with ozone-oxygen and the tips of those new red skis.

It was fairly glorious.

I hardly knew it had happened until, bingo! into the warm black velvet nothing of my mind there seeped, there stole, there slid, a line of a cheekily sultry poem; a nice surprise; I'd been wanting one.

And then, bingo! again; into my mind seeped the answer to all the world's sorrows. But it left me again, I am sorry to say; and so, like a dream, I lost it.

Next, it was a song I had made as a child and had long since, long since, forgotten. But I was happy to sing it again now, for it fit the rhythm of the slide-kick-slide of the skiing.

Now, it sometimes takes me a while to catch on to what is going on, in my own mind as well as in the real world. But when I began to see the pattern of things, and that there seemed to be another part of me, or another part of my mind, that was better equipped to run things than I was, why, I began to take unfinished business along with me on my walks, and let that mind finish it for me: to write poems and songs and letters, and make plans and revise them, and tell people off who had hurt me and then make it all up again so that we both/all were happy. So it got to be that by the time I got home again I had more than red cheeks and healthy lungs, I had saved myself a lot of time and trouble by going walking.

Well, once I didn't. Of course, this thing I'm going to tell you now happened some time ago, happened before I had learned to let my freshly aired mind do most of the work of daily living. Maybe it would turn out different now. I guess I sort of hope so.

As I may have said, a time or two, I live on the very tail end of a little town (or on the head end, on days when I am not feeling humble). I live right next to open fields of alfalfa and brome. And now and again, in the growing season, I may walk in the fields, but I mostly do not; I walk on the roads once the snow is gone; I don't want to tromp down a man's fine alfalfa.

But the trouble with walking down a road is this: I only seem to get so far before some farm truck stops and says, "Goin' far?"

Or at least the driver says it. And I generally say, "Just walking to walk, thanks," and that's it.

But one day I bethought myself: "*This* is not expanding the old horizons! There must be a million or two new people living hereabouts, what with the back-to-the-land-on-a-nice-sandy-acreage movement and all. I hardly know a single one of them. And the body is made so that I can walk *back* as well as I can walk *forth*, so why don't I just take a ride for a mile or two with the next truck (or person) to ask "Goin' far?" and see what I can hear from one of these new neighbours?"

So I did. I went walking. And sure enough, pretty soon a red Ford half-ton loaded with hay bales stopped and said, "Goin' far?"

And I said, cool as a cucumber, "Just a couple mile up the road, is all."

"Why, my goodness, hop in," he said. "Glad to have the company. Hope you don't mind the goat."

Well, tell you the truth, I hadn't *seen* the goat, but as it happens I like goats OK, so long as I am not in charge of them and am not expected to keep them from eating the shirts and long johns off my washline. So I said, "Don't mind at all," and climbed in. And the goat got to licking my hands and knees for the salt, and the driver and I got to talking about goats and how he'd got this nanny to provide milk for an allergic infant. And we got talking about allergies and infants (about which I knew my fair share, having had two of each for nearly thirty years, although the infants no longer fit the pram and have been buying their own milk for a long time now).

The next thing I knew we were at the two-mile crossroads. "This is where I get off," I said. The goat was done with my knees anyway, and was slowly working up.

And the driver said, "Oh my goodness, now, you're not meaning to walk all the way to the Thomases', are you?"

Well, I didn't even know any Thomases lived down that road; I am not the kind who has come into this world equipped to make mental maps of her local environment. But I couldn't really say, "No, I'm going to turn right around here, as soon as you're out of sight, and walk back to town."

Which I was, and which you know as well as I do. But somehow, that day, to admit it to a man who had been so grateful for what I had to tell him about a goat *we* once had who was allergic to children, was like admitting to looniness. And my reputation is not too safe as it is, in that department.

So, instead, I said, "Oh yes; I do it all the time."

And *he* said, "Oh, goodness, I wouldn't think of it; wouldn't think of it; I'll take you; you just stay put."

And he did. Two miles out of his way (and mine). Four, counting the way back to the grid. He dropped me right on somebody's doorstep (presumably, the Thomases), and there he waved good-by, and the goat bleated adieu to my hands and knees; and they were gone, back the way we'd come.

No one was home. I didn't even get to find out who really lived there, and maybe a cup of tea and a chin-wag, which might have saved the day. I slogged the two miles back to the grid and the two miles further to town. And I thought very little for a while about adventure and about expanding the horizons.

Just before the turn-off a big van pulled up. I didn't know this fellow, either. He had a small pony in the back. The pony was wearing a white carnation behind its right ear.

"Goin' far?" asked the driver.

I was tempted.

Then, "About forty feet, is all," I said. My feet were flat enough to last me for a month. But I'd sure give a pretty penny to know where that carnationed pony was heading that fine spring day, while I was limping home to a hot epsom salts foot-bath and a good long sit-down in my kitchen rocker in Vanscoy.

THERE IS NO SUCH THING AS TOO MANY POTATO PANCAKES

Shrove Tuesday almost came and went this year without so much as a by-your-leave from me, and the only reason I didn't miss it altogether is because I asked some folks to come to supper; and my Aunt Anna said, Well yes, they might have come, except, too bad, it was Shrove Tuesday and she and Georgia had promised the family potato pancakes for supper.

Well, say, that was news to me. But I never batted an eye; it doesn't do to admit you are surprised about such things. I just told her I knew how to make potato pancakes, too; so what was wrong with having them at *my* house? So that was good; and that was that. We did.

I do know how to make them, too. At least I know how to make them my way. My way is to put in a little baking powder and to make lots. There is no such thing as too many potato pancakes. They keep. They also keep getting better. As long as they last: not long.

Those are the only rules I have about potato pancakes.

Nobody else I know ever puts in the baking power; the grated potatoes don't seem to need it or want it, and mine come out as flat as pancakes anyway, in spite of the leavening; but still, I have got my pattern set and so I do it.

Everybody else I know who has ever made potato pancakes knows about the second rule. There is no such thing as too many potato pancakes.

My Aunt Anna used to try to disprove it. She kept making more and more potato pancakes every time she made them, but her three children had taken, early, to running a competition as to who could eat the most potato pancakes at one sitting.

The prize was the last pancake. As my Aunt Anna learned to grate more potatoes and fry more potato pancakes, David and Lyle and Georgia just kept growing taller and taller and creating more and more capacity for them. She must have been mighty glad when they finally left home.

I would have been. I don't really like to make them, and I never had to, much. I married this man whose father was half-Irishman and I don't know what it is about the genetics there, but that particular bloodline only wanted its potatoes boiled and served whole or maybe mashed; but they could never take to German potato pancakes.

I like less than ever to make them now, now that I have sent my heavy old food chopper to a house where it will be used often and admired much. Grating enough raw potato on a hand grater to make enough 'cakes to go around takes a long time, and so I seldom do it now.

If you want to know how to make them, it's easy. You take your pan of raw, grated potato and drain the water off, somehow. I don't care how you do it, short of using a clean bed sheet; that would be foolish. You can save that water back, if you want, for making soup or bread; only look out, it gets blackish looking and that may surprise you. (The bread never minds, though; especially if you make brown bread.)

Next you add a handful of flour. And you add four eggs, no matter how much potato; you can be very casual about potato pancakes. (Another rule you could have is: It is awfully hard to *spoil* potato pancakes.)

Add also a little dab of sugar and a quite a bit of salt. It is pretty hard to get too much salt in potato pancakes. (That is *not* another rule. It can be done. And it is not good. So let us say you will add half a teaspoon of salt for every two cups of grated potato, back there when you first started. Back there after you have drained the potato water off, only not using a clean bed sheet—which means *any* kind of bed sheet.)

You might need a little milk. It all depends. The batter can be runny. It doesn't care. So it's best not to pamper it.

That's about it. If you are going to make them my way you can add about an even teaspoon of any kind of baking powder; if you are going to make them my mother's way and Aunt

Anna's way and the way of everybody else in the world but me, you will not add anything more after the bit of milk: you just stir it all up together and then you are ready to fry the pancakes.

Don't forget the lard or dripping of bacon grease to help the frying. Potato pancakes stick; they have no mercy that way; but if you lace the pan with lard first they will nicely oblige you.

They don't mind how long they stay in the warming oven after frying, while you cook enough for ten people to eat supper together rather than in shifts, like you might have to do with high-rise pancakes. The poor folks from the old peasant days knew what they were doing when they invented cheap, unspoilable, almost-as-good-as-porridge potato pancakes.

You can serve potato pancakes with sausage or bacon or ham and eggs, if you want to.

My Aunt Anna says, when my Uncle Bill taught her to make them nearly forty years ago he taught her to make them the old-fashioned way: with potato pancakes you serve potato pancakes. But even that way, potato pancakes need chokecherry syrup or maple syrup or Roger's Golden Syrup or at least some kind of syrup—although anybody who knows anything at all about it will tell you that chokecherry is best.

When I was a kid we maybe had potato pancakes for supper on Shrove Tuesday, but I can't remember. I don't think there was a rule about it at all. I think likely on Shrove Tuesday we had anything that was left over from dinner, or was handy.

I am sure there are more important rules for Shrove Tuesday than having some kind of pancakes for supper, and I am also pretty sure that at one time I knew all those rules. I mean, I was born German Lutheran, and they don't mess around with things like that: when the pastor asks, you'd better know, or else!

I don't know any of the rules now. And somehow I know I am not going to give myself a refresher course either. I seem always to forget, nowadays, what the encyclopedia has told me, if I try to do that; I only seem to be able to remember what already has got stored away in my mind.

As for example, I remember Good Friday always seemed to be black and fitful and glowering, somehow, when I was a kid. Dark clouds. Rain. Snow. Both. No sun. And the wind was always scolding those who had killed the Christ.

My mother always baked hot cross raisin-spice buns on Good Friday all the years I lived at home; or all the years I choose to remember. If it had not been for my mother and those hot cross buns, when I was young I would not have been able to live through Good Friday. The least they could have done, I always used to tell myself, racing to bring the cows in before it rained or the wind tore you into two riven pieces, was to call it Black Friday and be honest about it.

It is a black day even today, if it is the day someone crucifies your wish to never die.

Easter Sunday was always fresh and cheery and golden. I don't know how my mother and The God of All Things managed to do it, but I remember Easter Sunday as always a pleasure (and maybe a relief that it was not yet *your* turn to die). You heard a lot about dying, during Lent and Easter, among German Saskatchewan Lutherans, in the early 1930's.

You heard a lot about resurrection, too. But somehow, after you had seen a cow or pup or your nice, white-haired opa die, and had prayed earnestly that they be made alive again, but they weren't, why, it was easier to believe in the dying part, and to wonder when it would be your turn; it was a whole lot harder to believe in the part that said you would arise again. It took me nearly fifty years to learn to believe it.

People go at it the wrong way, it sometimes seems to me. They pretend it has to do with church and goodness and God and the Lord Jesu or the Lord Buddha. (And some people have gone about as far as they can possibly go if they agree to throw in the Lord Buddha along with the other "good" stuff.) They say you have to follow the rules — at least in a general, or maybe even a loose way, like you do in making potato pancakes — and they say you have to follow the rules or you just won't make it back up out of the grave.

They all want to help you, of course. So they put those rules all together, nice and neat and handy, in catechism and Bibles and 4,000 Upanishads (same thing), and pretend it's the rules that matter.

The truth is, it's even easier than with potato pancakes, for there is only one rule.

Maybe I shouldn't give it, but I guess I'm going to anyway. It's just another natural, unchangeable principle, like the revolution of the stars or the ebb and flow of the tides in the oceans of Planet Earth: it is as impossible for the mind-spirit essence to die as it is impossible to hold back the tides or to stop the sun from doing what it has been doing since long before man learned how to deny.

I would have to write you another Bible to even come close to explaining how I know this; to tell you how I, an unbeliever for nearly fifty years, was finally given to believe.

Easter is nice, but it won't really do the trick, if you are not there already. The Lord Jesu and Buddha are lovely, but they are not the whole answer, and likely not half of it.

The way to know you will never die is to sit quiet, alone, and talk to your own mind, and so let it lead you, slowly, fearlessly, through the confessions and the sins and the fears and the Oh-I-can't-believe-thats. It takes a lot of years for some of us. But when you finally hear it from your own mind you will know, and you will never again disbelieve.

We have come a long way here from potato pancakes, or so it seems at first flush. Unless you consider how many lives it would take for true pancake lovers to get enough bacon bits-and-chokecherry syrup-laden pan-browned potato pancakes.

THEGARDEN

I don't know what it's like where you come from, but on the Saskatchewan prairies, where I come from, there are three things we do not joke about in public because they are personal and private — and because God or Allah or Fate or the pastor is gonna clip your future wings for you if you do.

The three verbotens are not sex, politics, and religion. Oh my, no. Sex, politics and religion we make fun of here all the time. You don't need sex, politics or religion to get you through hard times and 30 below winters (although you would never know it to listen to all the jokes lately about the sex part); all you need is *Thegarden*.

Thegarden is one of the three sacreds of the Saskatchewan prairies: one of the three things we never joke about in public (or even in private). And it's not because we're 99 and 44 one-hundredths per cent English out here. There are more Germans and Ukrainians than there are British in Saskatchewan and, as a rule, you don't really hear so many songs and poems and stories about German and Ukrainian gardens as you do about the English.

Still, English or not, we are garden crazy here in Saskatchewan.

Our population isn't very English, and our gardens aren't, either, full of posies and lined by clipped hedgerows and with a short row or two of cucumbers and lettuce and parsley liberally laced with forget-me-nots lending shy colours and a little artistry to all that plain old edible green.

In Saskatchewan we call the garden Thegarden, as though it was just one word, like Dandelion. One word, like Father-

SonandHolyGhost was when you were a kid and it was getting dark already out in the pasture and you had to bring the cows in right past an old Indian's grave. It didn't matter which was old, the grave or the Indian or both—when you went by it and it was nearly dark you said FatherSonand HolyGhost as if it was one word.

And that's how Saskatchewan people talk about Thegarden.

Some people gave up on FatherSonandHolyGhost back there in the Dirty Thirties. They got by instead, on their sunbaked, grasshopper-infested and hailed-out farms, because they had a cousin with a garden up in northern Saskatchewan where it always rained plenty, even in The Thirties. And people who had no north Saskatchewan cousin with a lush garden and plenty of potatoes and turnips to spare, hauled water in wooden barrels and poured it onto the plants with a dipper to keep Thegarden alive.

I sort of hate gardens.

Not Thegarden, though. That's quite a different thing.

Gardens are what I have to plough and sow and weed and harvest and can and freeze and store. Thegarden is what I can talk about and write about and feel good about. Thegarden is a symbol of something that comes very close to being God.

Gardens that I plough and sow and et cetera are about half an acre, and they are orderly and neat, or else! The strawberries are not allowed to run around in it. The peas grow, row by row, with their skirts hanging decorously over page-wire fences rather than tossing this way and that in every fresh breeze. And marigolds and cosmos do not lace their blooming way through *my* garden amongst the cucumbers as they might in an English one. They jolly well grow in rows or this spear maiden resorts to a sharp hoe to create a little order.

Gardens, for me, tend to take a lot of patience, especially when you add mosquitoes and wasps, and hedges waiting to have their out-of-shape bodies lopped back to svelteness even while the weeds are growing half an inch an hour in the tomatoes and corn. Mosquitoes and wasps want to be always where you are. I bought a bug zapper once, and it spoiled the robins unmercifully. They wouldn't bother to look for worms for breakfast; they would simply fly out to the bug zapper and patrol the ground below it for their protein. They got so they could hardly waddle home after breakfast, let alone fly, but I ditched the bug zapper when I discovered it wasn't doing much about zinging the mosquitoes; it was putting out of commission thousands and thousands of harmless but dumb May flies.

When it comes to Thegarden, though, oh my, I can wax as eloquent as the kitchen sampler in my neighbour's house down the block, said sampler avowing in Olde Englishe scripte that you are nearer to God in a garden than anywhere else on earth. (That includes certainly, I assume, any hot-as-hell, cramped, downtown studio where the television preachers are holding forth.)

And then there's ThegardenofEden, of course. God must have gone for a long walk, I've always thought, the day Eve was left on her own hook and so got hooked by the serpent of all-knowledge. (And Adam was out to lunch too that day, it seems to me, for he did precious little to preserve the innocence of his ostensible right rib, nor Thegarden as it was: a safe, pretty, cool, lush haven for green innocents who have no need to question. Or to learn.)

For my part, I've never had the experience of planting parsnips in ThegardenofEden, and serpents tend to steer clear of a fighting spear maiden, in any case, lest she lend them a hoe to the forelocks or hand them a ditto with instructions to weed the sweet corn.

I've never blushed amongst the red roses in a cool green bower, either, waiting to be plucked by a dashing poet prince who would dare to scale the moss-and-thorn-hung walls of Thegarden called Love-in-bloom.

I must confess that Thegarden of song and story and psychology I am much partial to, nonetheless. But of the gardens I have had under my jurisdiction to sow, to hoe, to harvest and preserve and pickle and store I have had a decided sufficiency, thanks.

I think maybe the only thing I really like about gardens I have had in my charge is *Thecrow*. There is currently one of the very large and very black variety that guards my Saskatchewan strawberries from marauding robins, and so I revere him.

I'm not the only one, you know. We do not make fun of

Thecrow in Saskatchewan. We may laugh at God and politics, and we very often do. God laughs at us, too, out there, jumping across our stubble like so many addlepated gophers, so that makes us even. But bad cess to any man who so much as smiles when he talks about Thecrow.

Or, heaven forbid, kills it deader than a newly transplanted green seedling in a bake oven noonday sun. "A murder of crows" is a lovely, lovely bit of wordage that satisfies the heart and mind and tongue as does "a gaggle of geese" or "an exultation of larks", but the murder of Thecrow by table thumpers in Thehouse — that rowdy (if not, indeed, bawdy) house built of fine stone and of masked words and set in the deceptively peaceful Ottawa Valley — the murder of Thecrow, I bet a purty, has done more to separate this country than all the free trade you can drum up or any amount of French you can force on a cornflakes box to sell in Ituna, Saskatchewan.

There's a third thing that's held sacred in Saskatchewan: *Thehouse.* (No, no, no, *not* the one in the Ottawa Valley!) Along with it comes *Thewife,* so we don't bother saying we have, as a matter of course, *four* things sacred in Saskatchewan. We believe in economy here because we learned thrift in the Dirty Thirties, so Thehouse and Thewife get lumped together, and neither of them seems to mind.

It's funny, in a way, that we seem to have these English notions out here in multicultural Saskatchewan. For just as an Englishman's home is his castle, a Saskatchewan man's home is his hotel. A Saskatchewanian has to take everything always one step further than an Englishman, or he isn't satisfied. He wants everybody in the world to feel free to put up there. Even if he's not going to be home. It will all be OK, he knows, so long as Thewife is there to make the beds and roast you a chicken.

Perhaps a scenario would be useful here. So, let us suppose you are not from Saskatchewan but that you have come to Saskatchewan this summer. OK? Well then, you stop a Saskatchewan farmer driving his tractor down the road, and you tell him you've got yourself lost trying to find your mother's cousin who's supposed to live around here someplace. The first thing that man will say is, "Irving Potter, you say? Why sure, you can't miss him, you just go about 3½ mile due south here and that'll take you up to Thehouse, and Thewife'll be there and she'll put the coffee on for you and phone Mabel Potter and Mabel Potter'll come on up to Thehouse and take you home."

Or let's say you drive onto his yard and you're selling cemetery plots in Kelowna or even vacuum cleaner parts. That man will stand there with a piece of tractor repair part in each hand and admire you and your car and your brochures for a minute, and then he'll say, "Good for you, good for you, tell you what—you just go on up to Thehouse and Thewife'll put the coffee on and look at all this stuff you got; she's canning peas, but never mind; you go on up to Thehouse, I think there's cake left too from last night's supper."

Thehouse in Saskatchewan is more than a shelter from Saskatchewan snow and dust and cold and wind; it is a comfort station and almost a temple, and Thewife is its comforter and its field marshal general and its priestess.

Thehouse . . . Thecrow . . . Thegarden.

But I have forgotten the most important point, I have a feeling. It has to do with Thecrow—the one that flies as a silent symbol over the gardens and the people of Saskatchewan.

Thecrow is a guardian, a shaman, a preserver: a god. Thecrow guards the soul, makes magic in the mind, holds safe forever the growing, glowing, glorious spirit of those who would believe.

A precious thing: Thecrow guarding Thehouse, Thegarden, always and always. As mine does, here in the little village that's called Vanscoy.

STRAWBERRIES

I hate 'em already. It's only May, and I hate 'em already. Strawberries.

Oh, I *love* STRAWBERRIES. Heaped red and large and luscious in a crystal bowl (or even a glass cheapie from Woolworth's); soaring blood-red and symbolic as all get-out in my mind's eye on days when the poet is in residence up there in the second-storeyed computer; titillating that other part of the mind with pictures of bowls of murky, muddy prunes—the old railway crews' "CPR strawberries". I am crazy about strawberries.

I am crazy about strawberries to think about and to make poems about, and to eat and to admire. But to tend them in a garden, when they do not know or even understand the discipline of order, why, that is getting to be beyond me.

Strawberries will not co-operate. Even though these are Saskatchewan strawberries, the strawberries in my big old garden here will not co-operate.

Instead, they run their wild gangly red-green feet this way and that in all directions. Even before the new age of Saskatchewan Born-again Private Free Enterprise, the strawberries in my garden went racing off to new and speculative adventures in the asparagus bed and the rhubarb patch and the corn; and even encircling—their wild warring tendrils boa-like and determined—the lone saskatoon berry sapling I've set such store by.

Strawberries know no discipline. They will congregate together, twining each other tight into one like-minded community (i.e. *snarly*) so surely that even in late April, showing hardly a snitch of green yet, their stubborn old-blood selves may be severed only at cost to you and/or the roto-tiller.

You can't kill them; they're like caraganas that way. You can't thin them out. You can't even slow them down.

Come the first spring rain they happily propagate new feet like twenty million brainless but prolific starfish giving Darwin a run for his money, and they set themselves to running all the harder to take over the entire garden.

A half-acre.

I mean, that's a lot of running-rampant strawberries, in anybody's book.

Suckers.

The feet are called suckers. Gardeners sucked in by pictures of luscious, dew-red strawberries on the back of a Nabisco Shredded Wheat box seven years ago, may now grab them up in a fury out of the corn or the asparagus and fling them wildly into the wind among the cucumbers and beans to suffer there in the sun until they die and fling their aura into that great strawberry jam pot in the sky. No matter. Two weeks later they've sucked enough food and water from the cucumbers and so there they are, large as life and busy as ever propagating more new feet.

When first I planted those suckering strawberry plants — a nice, neat baker's dozen (Aha!) — I swore I could never tire of the pleasure of communing with a patch of early morning strawberries. The first time I had to pick two dishpans full in one afternoon to save them from the sun and from the robins, I discovered what slave labour is all about.

I'd rather have been back picking rocks on the farm; they have machines nowadays to help you to do that. By the time I got all that strawberry jam made, I never wanted to see another strawberry again as long as I lived.

So the next thing I knew, I was saying so on the radio.

One of the pleasures of my life is to talk, now and again, on the radio. On the people of Canada's "local and regional" radio. And for some reason I've not yet been able to calculate, but am really pretty happy about, I am permitted to whine and moan and extol and complain about virtually anything that hops into my hermit mind on the taxpaying people of Canada's "local and regional" radio.

An awful lot of them seem to be strawberry slaves, too, because I got a lot of mail about that little talk about my revolutionary-minded strawberries. One or two did more than just commiserate; they helped.

One of the few heartening things, in this age of limited nuclear war talk and such, is to be reminded now and again how good people are to each other, if not to their governments. (And if governments were made up of real people, we'd soon solve that business of limited nuclear wars, I have a sneaking suspicion; don't you, now?)

Now, when I say I got some help from the empathetic general public, it didn't actually take the form, I have to admit, of folks showing up in my garden with sickles and hoes and pruning hooks to lop off the offending limbs of those Mongol hordes of strawberries forcing their way into the defenceless asparagus.

(Asparagus is not only defenceless, it is upright. Moral and upright. It just darn well stands there on its principled feet and does nothing, especially in dry weather; but if it moves at all, it moves straight up.)

The help I got from other Saskatchewanians also afflicted with strawberries was in the form of good and sensible advice. We're very good at that sort of thing here in Saskatchewan — where people are always wanting to help each other.

And of all the help I got over the matter of non-limited war on suckering strawberries, I suppose the most appealing came from John V. Hicks of Prince Albert.

Now John V. Hicks is not only one who has suffered under the hard rule of a strawberry patch, he is a poet and a bell-ringer and a musician. He is also the official and non-official poet laureate of Prince Albert. (Which just goes to show you, they have their heads screwed on right, up there in the north country.)

John V. Hicks has suggested rolling down an acre of 5-mil plastic (seeing as how I say I have a half-acre garden), and then cutting out a half-acre circle in the middle of it, and then digging

out all my strawberries from under the apple trees and in be-
twixt the corn and the beans and the dahlias, and planting them
inside that circle.

Then, says John, when the strawberry feet start to running, there'll be no place to run to (or on) save that black 5-mil
plastic; and—especially if it's wet and/or you've spread some
fresh banana peels around, they'll slip on their smart alec heels
and get set back on their a-a-a . . . adventures so fast they
won't know what hit 'em.

Now, isn't a brain that could devise such a solution, almost
altogether marvellous? It gives you some hope, and a whole
lot of comfort.

Strawberries. They're red. They're dewy-red sometimes,
and spotted with golden speckles. They're juicy and sweet all
the time and marvelously good for the body. They're nature's
ambrosia, and that's for sure, or else you wouldn't have to fight
to get them away from the robins.

I think there may be one small pot of jam left in the freezer.
You know what? I think I'll go fetch it up, and a loaf of light bread
baked just yesterday. And I'll have maybe seven slices of fresh
bread and jam when I come back in again from cutting the feet
off those garden strawberries.

ANNE OF GREEN GABLES, LIBRARIES, AND ME

When I was a kid, way back there in the Neanderthal times of the early 1930's, we had this library in the little country school I went to, about the size of two apple boxes. I mean to say the *library* was the size of two apple boxes, the *school* was about the size of a small box car.

Nowadays, when it is Library Day in this little town, I can look out my west bedroom window across to the new million dollar-and-then-some elementary school and see parked there the Wheatland Regional Library's book trailer, and it is larger than our *school* used to be back in those old days. Or at least it is to me.

In Wheatland's bookmobile you can not only get books, you can get tapes and records and films and micro-chipped this and that, and maybe even car tires and a brown bag lunch if you ask. I never ask. I'm happy with books.

In those old school libraries, like the one in our little Saskatchewan sandy hills school, there'd be maybe twelve out of the twenty-four original *Books of Knowledge*, 1914 version and pretty tattered; so lucky you if you didn't have to use the Index, it wasn't there any more; it likely found its way down the boys' toilet hole twenty years ago when somebody was up to some hellery.

And there'd likely be a full twenty-four volumes of *The Oxford Encyclopedia of Veterinary Medicine,* leather-bound in cowhide and as new as when it came over in insulated packing boxes from England. It was likely donated by the widow of some Remittance Man who'd got sent out by his family to start over with a clean slate in Frontier Saskatchewan, but who died before he could get up the spit to wipe his slate off nice and clean, ready to start over.

And lucky you, too, if you never had a hankering to look up Grease Heel or Glanders, because the page beforehand held the picture of a pot-bellied pony mare with crossed eyes and two heads — and how's *that* for an edifying education on a fine May morning when you are seven and allowed for the first time to go to the library and choose your own book?

And in the *other* apple box of that little library — I suppose I should say, on the other *shelf* — there'd be maybe a copy or two of *The Old Greek Myths* and one of *Blackie's Golden Annual for Boys,* and, if you were just awfully lucky, one of *Anne of Green Gables.*

I was crazy about Anne of Green Gables. It wasn't so much that she was Canadian that appealed to me — after all the Greek Demeters and Helens and after all the Penelopes who tagged along with their British brothers in *Blackie's Golden* — it was that Anne was as misfortunate as I was, and so we connected and were kindred spirits or anything else she wanted to say we were, even though I did not have red hair, I had white-blonde Lutheran German hair and I hated it because my mother kept washing it to keep it lovely.

Two short shelves of potpourri. Well yes, I agree, that wasn't much of a school library.

So, when my Uncle Emil came home from Clarkboro or Aberdeen with an armful of books for me from the newly-formed Wheat Pool Elevator Library (which had at least *seven* apple boxes worth of sweet, sweet books without a Grease Heel or Glanders picture amongst the lot of them), why, I learned to love my Uncle Emil and the Wheat Pool with a passion that has not diminished and which is not surpassed save by my passion for my Uncle Bill, whom I'll tell you about sometime, when I can bear to do it.

Then we moved to town. And in 1942, if you had ten dollars to spare you could buy yourself a library card for the Saskatoon Public Library and ride the bus four miles from the CPR town of Sutherland for a nickel and get all the books you could carry home in your mother's big old canvas shopping bag. I was crazy about all books by then, not just the *Anne of Green Gables*. But I never had the ten dollars.

Well, not quite so. These things are checkable, and so I'd better be right purely honest. I had it for about two years when I worked for The Bank of Montreal for sixty-seven dollars and thirty-two cents a month when I got out of high school. Two years of reading all I could read when I got done for the day confusing all I could confuse of the Bank of Montreal's figures.

Then suddenly it was 1950, and I'd got married to this big curly-headed country school teacher for some reason I can't now remember, and there I was, seven miles from any town, and closer to seven hundred from any library.

But lo and behold, The People of Saskatchewan had demanded (and been given) a regional library system just about then. And so, for free—for free, mind you—you could order books and get them shipped to you in the mail in a sturdy canvas sack the colour of sturdy new green oats—and they even sent you the postage to get the books back to Regina along with your order for fifteen more to devour by the next mail day.

All these many years later, the Saskatchewan Regional Library System is still intent on getting books to people like me who would die without them. But they also loan all those tapes and cassettes and records and films and micro-chipped this or thats I don't want to hear about, personally, because you can not cuddle a cassette, let's say, in your hands while you let your mind flow into it and its mind flow into you as you do with any good book. And they also loan, sometimes, at people's request, some Saskatchewan writer and talker who will come to their town for an afternoon or evening and talk about what makes a Saskatchewan book and a Saskatchewan writer, and then read them some stories or poems from just such a book to demonstrate.

I've got loaned to The People of Saskatchewan quite a bit like that, through the courtesy of Saskatchewan librarians, and I'll tell you I've almost always got my batteries recharged just by walking into a room full of people waiting to hear stories and poems about their own kind of people; the stories I hear from *them* when I am done talking are the bonus I always look forward to.

There was a time I was going so many places on behalf of Saskatchewan libraries that I almost got to feel like a librarian (the only thing in the world I have ever wanted to be, and which has been thoroughly denied me).

And just about then, there was the first-ever three-province librarians' conference at Jasper Park Lodge. And if Saskatchewan libraries, in their utter decency, didn't decide to trot along with them a crazy storyteller who just happens to be crazy about Saskatchewan libraries! Five hundred and two librarians and their board trustees all collected (along with fifty-six businesses all trying to sell them things) to tell each other more about the new technological way to run a library. I didn't want to hear any more about micro-chips and micro-fiches myself, they scare me too much, but I had just a whale of a good time, even if I did have to sleep for most of the night there in a clothes closet.

Everything was just so beautiful there at Jasper: the new books and the new and the not-new librarians; the posh lodge and the posher lake built by Mother Nature or The Lord of All things. (Take your pick; it all amounts to the same thing in the end.)

I simply refused to get any "hands-on experience" (librarians even *talk* different now than they used to) with the new "hardware" on display there, but it was sure a comfort to hear that something called the Inter-library Automatic Cataloguing System boiled down to mean it was a way to find you a book you want, fast, even if you're in Maymont, Saskatchewan, and the book is in the tardy clutches of a farming hermit sixty miles out of Hayter, Alberta.

I just turned my ears off at that and went for a walk around the lake, and when I got back I sat out on my own personal sun deck and admired my own personal view of Jasper Park Lodge and its lake.

If there was anything posher than the outside of both, it was the interior of the suite those librarians had allotted to their visiting Saskatchewan storyteller.

And still I slept most of the night in a clothes closet.

It wasn't that the bed wasn't comfortable. It was like sleeping on a cloud, I'm sure, if you could have got to sleep. But next door to me was a party (of *non*-librarians, I hasten to report) and it was long and loud and got louder and louder as it got longer and longer.

It was a summer of strikes, and next morning, very early, I had to be up to get the Alberta and the B.C. storytellers into Edmonton by a specified time on their crowded agendas. I get very tense about other people's crowded agendas.

I just couldn't sleep. I wasn't carrying enough aspirin to bed down even a mosquito and the medicinal brandy I carry along sometimes for just such emergencies seemed to have found another emergency somewhere along the line and what was left wouldn't phase out even a new-born gnat.

The clothes closet in that Jasper Lodge suite was as big as some bedrooms I have seen in town housing developments. It wouldn't quite hold the cloud mattress, though.

So I made a mattress out of blankets and pillows, and I made up a bed on the floor of the clothes closet, and I pulled the beautiful doors of it shut tight behind me, and I slept like a baby and was glad.

Next day we got to Edmonton in fine style and in plenty of time, and from there I practically flew home low, in the little Toyota Wagon I had then and loved with a passion that came close to the kind of love I have had for my Uncle Emil and my Uncle Bill and for Saskatchewan libraries.

ELECTION FEVER

Election fever gets to be an awful thing. I would rather have the Asiatic flu kind, or even malaria, for my own part. I see the darn thing heat up the body politic and the body political over and over again, and then simmer down and stash its hot little virus away, coddling itself in hot minds, ready to break out again in virulent form four or five years down the road.

For some years I was a village secretary-treasurer. But I took the job so seriously that I can hardly find it in me to find any humour in it even now, years and years later, and certainly none in the election stories I'd have to tell of those days. But I do remember a little election story from years that go back even farther than the days when I made up sewer bills and had to learn how to run municipal elections. (As soon as ever I could, I forgot how again.)

The little election story I remember goes back to when I was a kid on a little Saskatchewan farm. I think it is safe to tell it now, this story from years past, though it holds very little moral and even less accuracy. Historical fact has never been a strong point with me, you see; it has never turned me on as much as has philosophy.

I don't have a very efficient memory either; a computer memory deals you only efficiency, not amusing stories. But I do have a beautiful and forgiving sister, one who is pretty good at remembering stories from the old days in the same way I do myself and so I can tell you this little election story on me and on my sister.

My sister took a bribe and I didn't.

Now, she might remember this story the other way around.

If she does, she'll have to write her own book, or get up in front of people in public and tell it her way. This is the way that I remember it.

I am sure that I was the one who didn't take the bribe because I know that principle was so staunch in me when I was eight that it was suffocating. Let me tell you, in those days I was as moral as Saul once he'd seen the light on the road to Damascus, and so I wouldn't take the bribe.

And I have regretted it ever since.

This is how it happened: There was an election coming up, see, and we had a teacher in that little country school, there in the sandy hills east of Saskatoon, who believed staunchly in LEARN TO DO BY DOING. She believed in it so staunchly that whenever she said it you could almost see all the capital letters coming right off her tongue.

Anyway, in this case it meant we were going to have a mock election, ahead of the the real election, and learn how it was done by doing it.

Immediately this became known, of course, all the fathers and uncles and male cousins at home got in on the act. The women mostly stayed out of politics where I was brought up. They said it was all foolishness. They said politics was politics no matter its colour or its stripe, and there wasn't a government yet that they knew of that didn't in the long run stay a whole lot more interested in politics than it did in government.

So the women stayed out of it, but all the men got in on the act. And that had to be so, really, because if the Tories won the school election the Grits would all be mad as God in the Garden the time Eve discovered Truth inside an apple. If the Grits won, the Tories would be even madder.

And if the brash new C.C.F. won, look out, there'd be a war!

So there were all these fathers commanding their children to vote in the stalwart way their fathers had; and there were all these uncles bribing nieces and nephews to vote exactly the opposite.

So my father told us how we were supposed to vote in order to remain true Saskatchewanians (or true Canadians, I just disremember which). And one of our mother's brothers came up the day of the school election and promised us each two pounds of maple buds to vote another way.

Can you imagine two pounds of maple buds? Could you have imagined it when you were eight years old and living in a time when even a nickel Sweet Marie was something to remember for days and days? A whole two pounds of luscious, brown-as-brown, velvet-smooth, Dutch chocolatey maple buds, each one a perfect swirl of sweetness complete to the tiny hook at the top! Well!

My sister took the hook, but I didn't. I was too moral. To sell your vote, even for two pounds of maple buds that would last you for two weeks if you didn't share with anybody, say, that was as bad as spitting out Doktor Martin Luther's communion wafer when the pastor put it onto your tongue, or selling your soul to you-know-who.

But my sister did it. And our uncle's side won. And our uncle paid off.

And when he did, he said as plain as plain, because he was a sincere young man and believed he knew what was right and that he knew how to make others see things the same way, "But don't you share, now, mind you, with those who didn't vote right!"

And my sister smiled. She was always so darned cute and smiley, and I wasn't: I was just moral. And she took the two pounds of maple buds, it made a whole lot. And maybe she even kissed our uncle, I just disremember that, too, and it somehow seems important to be historically correct on that part, at least. Then again, he may not have been one of the kissing ones; and maybe it doesn't even matter.

What matters was my sister took the bag of maple buds, and smiled, and went outside into the sun; and I followed her, the smell of sweet swirled chocolate was a siren song I could not resist. And once outside she took my hand and we ran, ran, ran out past the house and chicken sheds and garden, to the safety of the maple trees in the lane. And she shared me maple bud for maple bud, the whole two pounds; and by suppertime we were both so sick we had a fever.

(I *told* you my sister had no morals!)

But I also remind you, *I* threw up as hard as she did; and

though I'd voted the right way and refused to sell my vote on principle, my mother spanked us both.

It's a funny thing: I suddenly feel like Aesop, the ancient story-teller from the old Alexandria Readers here. That means there must be a moral here somewhere, if I could only think of it.

Or thought it mattered at all.

NAMES, AND THINGS

If you happened to live in town when you were a kid in the 1930's or 40's, you may remember the Butter Woman who came to your place, Saturdays, to sell your mother butter which she liked better than what she got at the store, because it was better—or at least cheaper. The Butter Woman sounds like a very good name to call somebody if you read it in a book about "the good old days", or if you say it out loud. It has such a flavour to it, even if you say it to yourself inside, in your own satisfying mind.

The Butter Woman sounds like a good name to call somebody unless you are eight, and it is 1937, and it is the first time in a whole year you have got to go along to town in the buggy to see and do things, and if it is your mother who is called the Butter Woman by a sniggly Shirley Temple-ringleted kid half your size who has a smudgy face and the nerve to leave you and your mother standing at the open door whilst she hopscotches off to the innards of the house, yelling, "Mah-mah, The Butter Woman is here!"

You wonder, then, how your mother can smile and talk about the weather and Shirley Temple's mah-mah's front yard petunias, when Shirley Temple's mah-mah comes to the door to take your mother's cows' cream from her and counts twenty-five cents in nickels back into her hand.

Nowadays, I do not have to defend my mother's better name, and so I rather like the name The Butter Woman. Or The Egg Man. Or The Cream Lady. Maybe that happened after we got to living in town ourselves and The Milk Man came right to our door every day with ice cold milk in tall glass bottles which grew a little round glass cup at the top with a narrow neck, and inside which the cream collected so your mother could pour it off for your father's coffee or for the apple pudding at supper, before she put the cap on and gave the bottle a few upside-down flicks – your heart always stood still while she did it lest her finger slip off the cap holding the milk in whilst she flipped it, lest the milk swoosh clear across the kitchen floor, as it did the only time *you* ever tried it and so lost your mother twelve whole cents – to say nothing of the aggravation of wiping it up off everything including your baby brother and his bib and his teddy bear and his high chair where he sat banging his spoon for milk for his porridge and got it, surprise! right in the open kisser. (Which did not seem to stop him from yelling for milk again next time, but which seemed, at the time, a kind of a good thing to have happen.)

It's not the good old days anymore; it's the good nowadays now; and The Cream Lady I get whole cows' cream from yet, now and again – say at holiday time when there will be others around to help me get fat on it – The Cream Lady I know and love is called Mrs. Pierce and she lives near Pike Lake and tells you stories whilst ladling thick yellow cows' cream from her plastic ice cream pail into one of your mother's forty-year-old glass milk bottles. Mrs. Pierce has lived on the hill where she lives since years and years before the potash mine was where it is and spilling its secrets, late nights, onto the pastures and the poplars and the chokecherries.

If you want milk, and not cream, from the Pierces' cows, you have to talk to Mr. Pierce. Mr. Pierce is The Milk Man. And if you don't want any milk that day you had better look out, you might get something sweet and syrupy and appley in a large milk tumbler instead – and then you'll have to sit for another hour listening to more stories so that you can get yourself and that cream safely home to get fat on.

And even if you've sat that extra hour, Mr. Pierce's milk tumbler has likely been so big you are liable to drift just a little on the road home which ambles through brief hills and shallow dips larded with poplar bluffs and the new houses of new country dwellers and the older houses and barns of those who have farmed there for years and years.

And you get to thinking, somehow, about the name Farmer, and how, when you went to high school in Saskatoon with your own farm days hardly behind you, the young men and young women there called each other "You old farmer!" when they wanted to make a point about the cluelessness of the one who was getting called that.

And you pleasantly marvel to yourself, just sifting/drifting home through farming country that now holds more commuters than it does farming folk, that of all the names that say what people are and what they do — teacher, mechanic, miner, business tycoon, politician, priest, — you like the name Farmer best.

You have always loved the farmer the best.

The farmer farms. The farmer, man or woman, is husband-man to the life-giving land.

The farmer sows into the land, and garners from it, and then replenishes it so that he may sow and garner again. Farming is the most direct and immediate communion of man and the earth. Even man the hunter, back in the caveman days, was one step removed from it, for he communed with creatures one step removed from the earth, as he was; creatures who lived off the land themselves and so were somehow required, by the nature of things, to sacrifice their living bodies to this other creature who sprang at them with a long sharp arm which left his body and found them where they cowered in a thicket unseen even by the prime goddess, Sun.

It's a far remove today from early hunting man and his spear seeking a fallow deer in a gorse thicket as yellow-gold as his tawny hide. It's a far remove from that to combines and tillers and tractors as big as three caves; to computerized farm accounting; to mined fertilizer layered so thick onto tired soil you can see it again lying in ditches and gulleys after the spring run-off.

But to someone of my age and of my inclinations, a farmer will be a man or a woman like Mr. or Mrs. Pierce, who sow and garner and replenish the land now very much as they did when they began to farm it those many years ago. Before the mine's secret spillings were killing off the poplars and the chokecherries; the chokecherries which once grew so lush and so low the Pierces' cows got cramps in their several bellies from stripping off the tart purple fruit with long and yearning tongues.

I should have asked if the cream came out pink or purple, those times. I must find out the next time I go to call on The Cream Lady there on the hill near Pike Lake those several lovely non-kilometered miles from my house here in Vanscoy.

COMPUTATIONS AND SPECULATIONS

It is the age of the computer, and I do not like it.

Of course, I have learned long ago, to my regret and sorrow, that not liking something is no guarantee I shall be removed from it; that I shall not have to see and smell and taste and hear about it; that I shall not have to suffer pain or sadness (or computers) just because I do not like them.

It's not because computers are cold, hard/hot, metal that I do not like them. I have a little flying Japanese eaglet which is the same thing and I love it with a passion I once reserved for young men. I have even known some people who were as cold and hard as that kind of metal and it has been the cold, hard discipline of my life to understand, if not to love them.

The thing I do not like about computers is that somehow I do not trust them.

If computers came onto Planet Earth whole and complete and stillborn, and were then brought to life by their own cold, hard minds, not spanked into life by some flesh-and-blood hand of some homo sap master mechanic, I believe I would like and trust them.

If computers lived forever on their own cold, hard/hot, hard disciplined energy instead of having to be fed by human hands, I believe I would like and trust them.

If computers gobbled your bank deposit without the laying on of human hands to hurry the digestion, I believe I would like and trust them.

If computers pitted their own cold, hard/hot, hard reflexes against the cold-hot-hard reflexes of flesh-and-blood creatures without having to be fed quarters taken sometimes from some mother's purse, I am pretty sure I could like and trust them.

But that isn't the way it all works. The computer age is really not the age of computers: that's the whole darn problem right there. The computer age is really, it seems to me, a further age of humankind caught up in an even tighter web of "don't care" and "hurry-hurry".

I don't really like to say it that way. It seems unkind, somehow, when you have not had the discipline, yourself, of learning to feed and court and cajole a banking computer or a games computer or a business administration's computer. But all the same, when I go into a bank nowadays, I go prepared. I take with me a look of the eye and a set of the mouth that pretends I do not really feel like a homely and pigeon-toed young farm girl every time I walk into a place that looks more like an art gallery than it does a bank. And I take with me also a duplicate receipt for my poor deposit or withdrawal to make sure I remember what the computer was fed that day, in case the computer forgets. Computers are all too human, you see, I have discovered. In the same way spears and guns are.

I am pretty sure I have a scenario to illustrate that, but I may be wrong. Things make sense to me when they don't to other people sometimes; it's the price you pay for living alone and talking mostly to yourself; you and your Inner One develop a rather peculiar kind of logic and it is hard to see, sometimes, that in the Real World it doesn't make as much sense as you think it does.

Anyway, there are now games computers in some Saskatchewan schools, did you know that? That both surprised and pleased me, when I first saw it. But the thing is, when I go into a school, as I have done, and see a games computer sitting out in the hall, armed with Star Wars and Pac Man and expecting no quarter, if you see what I mean, when a young fighter engages it in combat, why I am reinforced in my notion that if computers were left to themselves to be born and to grow, we could like and we could trust, and we could even maybe love them.

Because, you see, there wasn't so much as one human being

stopped at the games machine. It was free; it was available. It was recess . . . and yet no one was stopped at the games machine.

So I somehow had to wonder: Is it the cold, hot, hard mind and heart of the computer that people are challenging when they stand in those arcade rooms and pull levers? Or is it the other world, the somehow lesser "real" world, which demands that they come up with cold, hard, coin of the realm before they are allowed to put their minds into play?

That sounds pretty down-beat, I suppose, yet I am pessimistically cheerful, if you know what I mean, and I have this sure (though, odd) belief that someday a computer will be born, in a lowly stable somewhere, to save us from our human selves. In the meantime, here we are, stuck with all-too-human computers in a sometimes less-than-human world, a world that changes too darn fast to suit the likes of me.

In the world I used to know better than I know this brand new hardwared and fast-moving one, it was different. I knew that world better because I did not live by myself and into myself; I went out into the world to earn my bread and butter—or at least my board money, for my mother fed her bed-and-board working children better than bread and butter at her efficient meals. And in those slower times those who stood on the seller's side of a shop counter did not talk about the Tupperware shower they had been to the night before to someone else on their side of the counter, whilst reaching a casual palm in your general direction there on your side of the counter for your money to ring into their mini-computer sitting there on top of the counter where a good, big, strong, sensible cash till ought to sit, and which rang a little bell every time it was punched open to alert you to the fact that your change was about to be counted back to you.

In those days the people on the seller's side of the counter used to talk to *you*, and say things like, "Now, if it doesn't fit, don't hesitate to bring it back and we'll get our lady in the back to adjust it for you—no charge, of course." Nowadays, people on the seller's side of the counter talk *to each other,* or else they talk to their mini-computer, which talks in a loud voice and tells the whole world you have bought only items from the No Name economy shelf again, though all those lined up behind and beside you have been courting the import shelves and the Canada Fancy grades as usual.

In the world I used to know better, nobody in the business of selling ever told you if you didn't like it you could go someplace else, except maybe in the War years when you were offered a secondhand tire for the price of a new one because the seller knew there was no place else for you to go. But he always smiled when he said it, just as if he was still trying to help you, when he said, "Well sir, maybe you should just let it go by. Maybe you'll just happen to catch one in Regina sometime, eh, if you've got yourself a way to get there?"

I'm not saying there was nothing wrong with that slower and uncomputerized age. There was the War, for one thing. And I'm certainly not saying the reason the people who are paid to sell things nowadays sometimes don't seem exactly one hundred per cent ready to "service" you is just because there happens to be a mini-computer sitting on the counter between you. Even my peculiar logic won't accommodate such a weird notion.

No, it somehow goes deeper than that.

It has something to do with the fact that a computer is a tool, I have a notion, so most of us stand in awe of it, just as the buyers of the first arrows and poison darts must have stood in awe of that earlier magic and so they did not think to question the motives of the human who peddled them.

The business world — the marketplace — is still, in the long run, simply a place where goods and services are exchanged for other goods and services. It has to do with satisfying people's needs. And the way it is done is what is somehow most important, it seems to me, if we are to be growing souls.

Bare bones essentials will do it; why not? Once it must have: "What do you need today, stranger? One large fish? Here's one. Will this do? Then give me three cowrie shells and it is yours." Bingo. Period.

In those times the fish likely tasted better than the communication, the coming-together of seller and buyer. But after a while, that wasn't good enough. Humans are social creatures, creatures of feeling. They are creatures of many different kinds of needs, not just the need for a fish to fill the belly. They are creatures who have needs of the spirit, too—though sometimes that need is simply to need more *things*.

That really doesn't matter. What matters is that certain sellers began to recognize things had surged suddenly past the point of simply barter, or even simple buy-and-sell. They learned to serve people in such a way that they wanted to come back, even if the fish were a little bigger elsewhere. And they used words to do that. Words. The most marvelous/dangerous tool ever fashioned by the species that somehow grew the biggest brain of all the creatures and so learned to walk at a ninety-degree angle to the ground, if he did not exactly learn to walk always staunchly upright.

(And if you see two meanings to the last word in the preceding paragraph, you know what I mean about the marvel and the danger in words, now don't you?)

If the seller walked upright in that other sense of the word, his/her part of a market conversation likely went something like this: "Good morning, good morning, good morning, Mrs. Ungava; a lovely morning, not? And what can I do for you on such a lovely day? A large fish for roasting? Here you are; how about this one? I heard you were having relatives again and I saved you this one, special. Two cowrie shells. Never mind, I know they were three cowrie shells every day last week, but my dear lady, company to cook for five nights out of seven, my goodness, you just take this—look, I got it already wrapped nice in bango-bango leaves—you take it for two cowrie shells and don't ask no questions and cook it in good health, and make sure you *eat* a little too, yourself; it will keep you in good health for cooking for all this company, may The High One preserve you from too much more of that."

If the seller didn't walk quite as upright as he might have, the words took on a kind of computer-like tone—which is to say, the conversation had no heart in it. "Mrs. Ungava. Well, well, well, company again, is it? Well, if this isn't your lucky day! I've saved back for you, special, this Extra Large Giant-Size snapper. Of course, it's Extra Large. It doesn't matter if it seems smaller than last week; *seems* doesn't count. This is guaranteed Giant-Size and only four cowrie shells, now can you imagine that? Well, of course it was three last week. What can you do? It's inflation. A man can hardly keep his head above water as it is. Sure, it's fresh. I don't care *what* its eyes say to you, it's fresh. It's a special kind of snapper, see? Just discovered. Brand new. And the eyes of this brand new, just-discovered snapper always look kind of stale like that. It's the way The High One made 'em, so as to fool their enemies, see? And if you take it right now, before somebody else comes along and wants it, too, so that we maybe — may The High One forbid — raise the price another cowrie shell, I'll even wrap it up for you in some bango-bango leaves so the bread fruit in your basket don't steal away the flavour."

Words — don't we all know it? — make an awful difference to the flavour of the service we get given to us. And somehow most of us know when the words are not just words: they are non-computered service, generously given.

Unless I am sorely mistaken.

HORSES, HORSE-COWS AND COWGIRLS

They say there are more horses on the prairies nowadays than there were in the 1930's, and who am I to doubt it? They say these horses aren't hauling ploughs and Sunday buggies, they're carrying rodeo cowboys and ranch-hand cowgirls, or they are jumping elegantly over stiles in horse shows; or else they're all standing around in pastures and paddocks somewhere waiting to do such things.

Well, I know from first-hand experience they are not ploughing the fields so that Saskatchewan can go on pretending it is the wheat basket of the world, because there are fields right outside my kitchen window which lets me see quite a good chunk of Saskatchewan so long as I do not let the caraganas grow too high. And so I know it is not plough horses but horsepower that is turning up furrows these days.

I don't know about any of the rest of it and I am not exactly dying to find out, but they say that horses are a classy business nowadays; and if I sound just a little sassy about it all maybe it will become clear later why I seem so.

Horses may be a business all right, and I am sure horses still *mean* business, as much as they did when my father had a pair who ran my sisters' lives and mine, for a couple of years back there in the 1930's. For horses nowadays won't even let you get on their backs and ride them unless you have taken (and paid for) lessons in how to do that.

Nowadays, to ride a horse you'd better have some style or else you'd better not bother; and there's a sweetheart of a woman I know who was born on a little old sandy farm, like I was, and she once explained her non-finesse as an equestrian by saying, "Listen, kid, you can't develop a helluva lotta style riding bareback on a plough horse in the hot sun to fetch home your father's cows."

For my part, I never even had a horse, plough or otherwise, to fetch home my father's cows. But I almost had a cow once.

My father had mostly Holsteins. Dairy cows. But some were only Holstein as far as the black and white splotches on the hide. Some were mostly range Hereford with the red hidden, and some were mostly camel or giraffe, and all of them had long unHolstein horns. Why, he had this one horny Holstein heifer — he had this one horn-ed Holstein heifer, to be more precise — and let me tell you that Holstein had horns on her like a longhorn Texas steer straight out of a B movie starring the Sons of the Pioneers.

Her name was Skitter.

Skitter, though supposedly a Holstein, didn't have a generous pillow-sized, pillow-soft Holstein udder, not by any stretch of the imagination. She had an udder the size of four small teacups and spigots not bigger than a four-year-old child's thumb.

She was going to be a devil to milk. So my father just kept on letting her be a heifer.

And Skitter's horns kept growing, though her udder didn't. Her horns got so big and so long and so handy it just struck me one day, when my feet were so sore from chasing cows home for milking: supposing I tried to ride that heifer? I wouldn't need a rope nor a halter nor a bridle, I could just steer her by the horns like a bicycle. (I didn't own a bicycle, either, mind you, but I'd seen one or two and I knew they had handles.) If I'd had a bicycle, I wouldn't have been trying to make a cow into a riding horse.

So I used to grab those bicycle handle horns and vault myself atop her like a cowboy at the rodeo. But she'd just give a casual swipe of the head, like she was brushing off flies, and there I'd be, a downed cowgirl. So I took to catching her near the pasture fence and I'd scramble up it, but about the time I was ready to mount she'd move off, grazing as she went, and I'd mount the ground instead.

Then came a time I had to start taking my kid brothers along for the cows. To train them, or something; I just disremember. And I figured if *I* couldn't get to ride, why, one of them should.

So I grabbed up my brother Eddie; he was smaller, though good at yelling "I don't want to!" all the time, which made you give yourself the discipline to make him do things anyway. And I swung him up on Skitter's back, fast. And then, talk about a rodeo, you should have seen the action.

He didn't get killed, though; there was hardly any blood at all. And neither of my little brothers ever told on me, even when they got to be a whole lot bigger than I was. But they threatened to, whenever I so much as mentioned riding Skitter again. And then next thing I got moved up a rung in the ladder of farm chores or something, and the boys got set to fetching the cows home alone.

And I still can't ride a cow or a horse to this day. Any style. Especially bareback.

Now, I know it's likely kind of hard to believe that kids could grow up on a Saskatchewan farm in the 1930's and not learn how to ride a horse. I just wish you had known some of my father's horses, and then you'd believe anything. My father's horses could have and should have ruined my regard for horses forever, or at least for life.

But they didn't. I love horses to see and to speculate upon and to admire — so long as they are not mine. There is something about them, something about their style that says, "I am free, do you not envy me?" even while they are enclosed in stout pastures or carrying stout passengers on their backs. And so I admire them, admire them all.

And I heard a snatch of talk on the radio here one day a while ago, saying there is a whole forest full of untamed and wonderfully wild horses some place in this country. I don't know where. On some Crown land somewhere — wouldn't you know it? It follows, because the other snatch of words I heard, just before I went out the door to scold some weeds in the garden, is that the Crown has decided to send those free and forested wild creatures to the canners — supposing the Crown can ever catch them.

The Crown, it seems to me, tends to be very good at deciding things like that. And spending time and money doing things like that. Or at least trying to do things like that. Or at least setting up commissions of one kind or another to try to get people to do things like that. For my money, the Crown and its costly machinery of human beings and their paper and their hardware has its work cut out for it to catch and can those lovely, free-style horses.

It was catch as catch can, with my father's horses. And I thought perhaps I was getting a direct-line message from my deep, dark subconscious about those horses maybe three days before I heard this bit of radio talk about the Crown's wild horses. I had a dream. In fact, I wasn't even asleep yet when the dream came; and it was filled with full-and-living colour pictures of myriads of horses; of beautiful, flowing, careening, prancing, waltzing, milling horses, with the most marvelous manes and tails.

And three days later I heard about the Crown's unwanted horses.

I'm not as worried as I might be. I mean, as it stands, already The Lord of the Order of All Things may be seen to be working in favour of the horses. Or at least it is some marvelous happenstance that the winter had been so mild, in the Crown's first crack at the job of playing trapper, that the horses were able to turn up their noses at the best hay taxpayer money could buy, and which had been set out on purpose to trap them.

They are swift, it is reported, and they are wily.

They are also, I bet a nickel, the direct descendants of my father's colts, Bob and Bing. (Yes, of course they were named after Bob Hope and Bing Crosby; my father was the kind of man who somehow had to do that.)

Bob and Bing were the wildest colts a little Saskatchewan farm ever grew — maybe even wilder than what has got grown so far in the Crown land forest full of wild, wild horses. They were beautiful: the golden-brown of well-baked bread, with marvelous heads and clear eyes, and with long full-swirling manes that made dance patterns when they tossed their heads in the yellow morning sun. But Bob and Bing had no consideration for anyone, and certainly none for my father's fences.

Those two could crawl or jump or bust down or wiggle through more fences than any adventurous milk cow who ever wore a fence yoke. (If you had a fence crawler, in those days, as you may remember, you made her a collar of four crossed lengths of wood; pole or flat lumber, whatever you had, it didn't matter. It looked like the pattern kids draw on paper to play X's and O's on, and some people called it a fence yoke.)

My father didn't put one on Bob or Bing, but he should have!

They refused to stay put. They were green-broke two-year-olds, born to speed and the Wanderlust. And as soon as ever my father set foot off the place they simply walked through the barbed wire as if it were mist and wandered off, hands in pocket, so to speak, and whistling.

Then my sisters and I would have to take off in three separate directions, on foot, (and wishing we had another sister to cover the fourth direction) to stalk them and fetch them home.

It was useless. As soon as ever they spied us they quit sauntering and took off, like Bellerophon's Pegasus, with a flying gallop.

They were generally fetched home by the neighbours.

And all of that is the reason I do not want a whole forest of horses killed and canned, unless *I* am the one delegated to do the chasing, in which case I may just change my mind about preserving the free spirit of the current likes of Bob and Bing.

And all of that is the reason I have this passion for horses as long as they are at a distance and with a good pasture fence or a whole forest between us.

And all of that is the reason, I suspect, why I dream most often not of horses but of Holsteins.

DEAR OLD SCHOOL DAYS; DEAR NEW SCHOOLS

Back-to-school Day came and went this year, and I hardly noticed it. I hardly noticed it, though Vanscoy's new million-dollar school sits right across the road from me, and all manner of loud yellow Hertz buses must have delivered all manner of young folk into that school's maw, or onto its environs one day here around the first of September.

I suppose I hardly noticed it because I no longer have chick or child or even a school teacher living with me to send off to school as I once did, with a sound breakfast under the belt — or the threat of a belt if the child kept complaining my kind of breakfast sounded a bit much; what he wanted to hear was the snap, crackle, and pop of prepared cereal and not the slippery slap of good honest porridge on his plate, if he had to eat at all.

I tend to be old-fashioned. That is pretty obvious, I imagine. I find old things and old ways comfort me. And change, now, is too often a big change. I used to look out the west bedroom window here and see a big and open school yard. Now I look out and see a big brown and black and hit'em-in-the-eye orange-yellow school spreading out over ninety per cent of what used to be school yard. And every time I look it surprises me.

That school went up so fast! I can't say it mushroomed, because it is as flat as a dinner plate. Maybe flatter. It sits there like all new schools across the prairies now sit: it sits all across the prairie — or across a whole lot of it, long and low and flat as the prairie it sits on.

Prairie architects seem to want to make awfully sure prairie folk keep "the unobscured horizon", it seems to me. We've made such a thing, maybe, of the prairie passion for seeing "miles and miles of nothing but miles and miles". Or else, it's just occurred to me, the architects of prairie schools are *not* prairie architects. If they are not, maybe they hate the prairie, for it can be quite forbidding if you have not been suckled on it. So maybe that explains why they give us schools so flat the first rain rains neatly through the half-a-million-dollar roof right off the bat.

Long low prairie schools, unless most marvelously insulated below those flat, flat roofs, must be designed to help warm up the long low prairie, when it's thirty-seven cold Fahrenheit ones below.

This new school in Vanscoy has been welcomed by almost everyone but me, and I'm sure there is a reason for that. It is said to be beautiful and efficient and I am quite ready to believe that, for it cost one million, six hundred and forty-seven thousand, seven hundred and fifty-seven dollars, and I don't know how many cents (although I'm pretty sure there were some). I know the whole cost, except for the cents, because "Saskatchewan Education" put up a big sign, right across the road from me, a sign almost as big as the school when it rose out of the prairie one night.

"Saskatchewan Education", if I remember right, used to be the Saskatchewan Department of Education, back in the days when we still tried to make words mean what they said and not what the person who makes up new names has decided inside his own head the name means.

Every morning, when I got up out of bed and went over to the west window to see whether (1) the world was still there, (2) we were having any weather this day, (3) Cominco was still there to the west, looking quite neat and lovely, actually, rather pinkish and whitish, and efficient and non-poisonous because it's so far away from my window—every morning, once that sign was up, I saw that sign telling me: SASKATCHEWAN'S FUTURE IS UNDER CONSTRUCTION AT A SCHOOL NEAR YOU!

Meaning me, I guess. Meaning somebody knew already I am the only person in this neat and peaceful and forward-looking little town who does not like the looks of a modern flat-prairie school.

They didn't have to tell me that school was under construction, though. Every day, before the sign even went up, I was picking litter out of the caraganas and cotoneasters on my place and even out of the strawberry patch and asparagus deep inside the bounds of the garden.

Well, maybe Saskatchewan Education *did* have to educate me: otherwise I might have surmised a Colonel Sanders had sprung up and I was being treated to the paper debris while the land gulls were marshalling forces to move in and pick the chicken bones clean.

Anyway, they told me. And it wasn't really news to me. What was news was, in the noble cause of "Saskatchewan's future", Saskatchewan Education felt free to deposit debris daily in my hedges and grass and garden. And all the while I collected it and put it into my own trash barrel I knew it was not Saskatchewan's future under construction near me, it was just another building.

Nobody can kid me. Saskatchewan's future is in its *people,* not in another million-and-then-some pancake school.

And when the people who used to run little Saskatchewan country schools were trying to make sure they'd build Saskatchewan's future with the help of the likes of me, we used to have field days to clean up the litter. A Spring-filled field day to clean up the winter litter; a Picnic day field day to clean up the summer picnic litter; a Fall field day to clean up the autumnal litter so that there wouldn't be so much winter litter to clean up at the next Spring field day.

We hated it, of course. The only good thing was if you had a teacher who let you use school time for the clean-up instead of making you do it after school. But it made us into the kind of people who cannot bear to have junk lying about our yards and flapping about our town, saying to passers-through, "Was that a town, or a pig-sty?"

Departments of education and their construction companies are made up of people, too. And they are part of Saskatchewan's *present,* whatever their future may be. And a present, doggone it, should be beautiful. Neat, and presentable, and beautiful.

And all the while this new school was being built I couldn't help but wish all those people, already trained in long low Saskatchewan schools and now busy building more of them would quit building half an hour earlier each day and have a quick field day to spare their neighbour and this town all that litter.

Well, it's cleaned up nicely now, and things look as neat as a pin.

And everyone else seems to like it, including the goers-to-school.

That's the one thing I like about this new school: it has brought the school-goers closer to my window. They come, flaxen-haired and brown- and black- and mouse- and auburn-haired, seemingly full of good cheer and willingness. The junior playground equipment has had to be more or less plonked down here and there because of this reason and that reason (one of which, I heard someplace, has, in a round-the-mulberry-bush way, to do with strikes). And nobody's had time to cut the heads off a summer's growth of weeds. But those active farm and town and country acreage kids are all over the place being happy and healthy and full of vim and good Saskatchewan vinegar.

If there is even a one who has crept like a snail unwillingly to this stark new glowering cracker box they call a school, why, he/she doesn't show up from the west bedroom window where I stand, mornings, to listen to them and to admire them. These children laugh and yell and whistle and shout and beller and Bronx-cheer with and for and at each other joyfully, just as we once did forty years ago, in a cold little pimple of a frame schoolhouse elsewhere in Saskatchewan.

And, no, the mention of those old horrors shall *not* make me change my mind about this new school. There is a happy medium between those first cold drafty oat bin schools and these cold flat oatcakes of today. It has to do with brick and A-frame roofs and beauty of form and of place, and I won't be drawn into talking any more about it just now, so don't ask, OK?

In the meantime, the kids I watch, mornings, from a west bedroom window, will do all right.

After all, they're born of the hardy prairies.

NOW, THOSE DARN TOMATOES

I was born in September, and a lot of other good things have happened to me in September since then. In fact, the only month of the year I like any better is May, when things begin to get green as green again, and to fill you with good hope and real gratitude that you've made it through another Saskatchewan winter.

But September could be a little bit better, if it tried. Or if I weren't so set in my ways that I tend to take the pleasure out of it by having dealings with those darn garden tomatoes.

I don't know how it is with you and where you live, but here in the village of Vanscoy where I live, along about the end of September, when my birthday is over and done, I generally have the titillating experience of trotting out to the garden at about eleven o'clock, with the night as black as the inside of a cat and with a weak-eyed flashlight and seventeen pails and assorted cardboard boxes, to pick the green tomatoes lest they freeze on their vines as I am freezing on mine whilst I pick.

At least they were green this year. In fact, by the time I had to save them from Jack Frost and from themselves, they were still as green as May grass. It's been such an odd-ball of a year that nary a tomato so much as pinked on the vine, let alone ripened to a hearty ketchup red.

This was the darndest year I have ever seen, and especially for tomatoes. The first of the darn things was to find any to plant. I should say to transplant. For I gave up coaxing seeds into seedlings a few years ago because I got tired of coming home from a few days on the road to find the little jiggers all dried up and roasted into frizzled black hair in their window boxes and in full combative view of the sun.

It became a pleasure to drop in at a supermarket just after the first full moon in June and slap down a dollar for a dozen plants and run them home and have their heels sitting in warm wet earth in no time flat – and no sweeping up of old manure and earth and peat moss if an elbow caught a tomato box bed on the way by and sent it all over the front room carpet.

But this year, you could hardly buy a tomato seedling for love nor money. Every gardener and his/her dog and grandmother was going in for tomatoes, people said, for California tomatoes were just too high to buy at the supermarket.

I finally found eight wizened and yellowing plants in a small flat that had got filed in with a tray of marigolds, though I found them a whole week after the full moon had been visiting my garden looking for some to bless. I was so happy to find these that I went out and planted them by Old Weakeyes flashlight the very same night.

Three went in head first, as I discovered next morning, but I resurrected them all like Lazarus and they dug in and grew as if it didn't matter a darn to them one way or the other.

You should have seen the bushes those puny little wisps had become by Dominion Day weekend; I was afraid to go out into the garden to weed without a machete.

At first there seemed to be no flowers coming, and so I sorrowed, for have you ever seen a tomato set fruit without them? Then, bingo! there they were – oodles and oodles and oodles of little green marbles hanging underneath all that foliage. The flowers had simply been in hiding in all that Brazilian forest jungle. So, there was the fruit on the vine, by George, and there'd be no California red, I thought, in the salads that got made in my kitchen that summer.

But summer came and went and there weren't any *Vanscoy* reds adding a bit of colour to the lettuce and cucumber, either. Those darn tomatoes just sat there, green and grinning, all August and most of September, and they didn't even have the grace to blush. Every time the kids came home to visit they talked about bacon and tomato sandwiches, and grilled tomato and green pepper omelettes, and a new red tomato to eat out of hand whilst wandering through the garden to congratulate the weeds on another successful year.

They might as well have talked about flying to the moon; they had a hundred and twenty-eight per cent better chance of flying to the moon than they had of seeing, let alone eating, a red tomato off the Vanscoy vines this unholy summer.

Came the first frost warning, I didn't even bother collecting sheets and blankets and old coats to cover that jungle; I just went out and gathered them in, green and hard and bouncy as new baseballs.

I just couldn't take it any more.

Tomatoes are supposed to grow *red* in my darn garden, and those that won't oblige won't get coddled under old army blankets around here anymore, not by this field marshall general.

I am learning to face facts in my ripened years. To analyze the why's and wherefore's of the idiosyncrasies of the Saskatchewan human race. And to profit from the analysis.

I don't mean to say I now give seminars — at forty dollars per attending brain — on "Psychological Dependency of Saskatchewan Gardeners on the Early-maturing Tomato." I mean to say I have satisfied myself sufficiently as to what those needs are, so that I no longer need them. The needs. Nor the tomatoes, for that matter.

I see it like this: If you have been through hard times, why, once the times get better you swear you'll see to it that you have more than enough of everything from then on — and that includes tomatoes: fresh tomatoes, canned tomatoes, frozen tomatoes, tomato paste, tomato ketchup, tomato chili sauce, tomato mincemeat, tomato et cetera, et cetera.

To have more than enough on the Saskatchewan prairies means you'll be safe for (and from) the winter. And so will your kids, their kids; your neighbours, their neighbours. For to be in a position to give generously to others the fruits of Mother Earth seems important to us as a people. You forget the hours of hoeing and the armies of cutworms and cabbage worms and aphids and ants and mosquitoes when you can offer someone a bushel basket of large, plump-cheeked, scarlet Campbell Kids tomatoes.

But dare I suggest there is an element of competition involved among gardeners reared on the mother's milk of the co-operative movement here? The Wheat Pool. Brotherhood-of-man medicare. Socialized auto insurance. Co-operation with a capital C. What does it do to them to so much as hint that the philosophy of Biggest = Best (and Earliest = Bester) has infiltrated the tomato patches of socialist Saskatchewan?

Yet, if it is not so, why is it, when I have strong-armed a visitor out to my tomato patch to show off the first dead-ripe succulent beauty of the season (and which I then offer to serve up, sliced, on the altar of . . . friendship? oneupmanship? . . . on said visitor's luncheon plate, said visitor says, as nonchalant as King Henry about to lop off another wife's head, "Oh yes, *we've* been eating them for a week at *our* place (exclamation mark). Aren't they nice and early this year?"

I may be wrong about all this, and I hope I am. I have to admit, there is something about the arduous nature of working a half-acre garden with hoes and long hours in the sun that affects the brain and the temper and leads readily to the addling of the brain waves and the growth of a hair trigger on the temper.

And tomatoes are, after all, sort of a scourge. So many things can go wrong with them: cutworms, "damping off" (a most curious condition with a most curious name that seems to mean you gave the darn things too much water and not enough heat in the seedling stage), too many flowers, too few flowers, aphids, hail, early frost. So the gardener who harvests great bushel baskets of fat red juicy Beefsteaks or Early Manitobas is harvesting the red badge of courage as well.

Those darn tomatoes look too beautiful to eat then, too beautiful for words, almost.

Yet people write poems about red *roses,* which do not perform too well in spaghetti or on toast, and they write those poems even here in ardently sensible and survival-oriented Saskatchewan.

SHEEP, SALTY AND OTHERWISE

I went, this year, to the annual Vanscoy Sheep Show and Sale, and somebody said it was about high time I got there.

The thing is, I live what we used to call "just a good spit" from the old Vanscoy Circle Hall (which was built with no corners so the devil can't catch you when you go there to dance and otherwise live it up in a loose and tempting manner), and I live no more than the same good spit from the new Vanscoy Curling Rink, yet I never seem to get there, either to curl or to outrun the devil, or to attend the annual sheep show. Which is actually held in the still newer Vanscoy Ice Skating Rink, but there, you have to forgive me a few lapses here, seeing as how I hardly ever get there to get them onto the map inside the head and so talk about them accurately when mentioning them at all.

I live such an insular life, in fact, here in my big old house on the very edge of town, that I didn't even know the first ever annual Vanscoy Sheep Show and Sale was going on, some years back, until I went out to fetch some rhubarb from the garden and there was this big determined-looking sheep standing on my backstep looking as though he meant to ring the doorbell.

Only I haven't got one.

And when I hollered for help and we tried to round up this sheep he simply stuck his head, horns and all, through the caragana hedge and stayed there. The more we pulled, the harder he pushed into that prickly old caragana.

"Just like a stupid sheep," I grunted, still pulling. "Just like a stupid old sheep."

But someone came along just then and told us that sheep belonged at the first ever annual Vanscoy Sheep Show to get sold, or chased by sheep dogs so the sheep dogs could show how sharp they were, or to get made into sheep-burgers, something MacDonald's has so far not thought of. So I decided right then and there that sheep was not so stupid: a prickly caragana hedge likely beat any of those things by a country mile, or by one point five darn kilometers, if you have to have it that way.

Sheep are not stupid. Lissa Sykes of rural Vanscoy runs only about twenty-five producing Dorset ewes, but every one of them, she says, is interesting, productive, co-operative — and bright enough to hide in a caragana hedge if she has to, to escape the meat grinder or a large-mouthed dog.

There seem to be more women breeders of sheep around Vanscoy than there are men. The women say they keep sheep for extra income because they live on marginal land, and sheep are rather fascinating, besides being small enough for even a small woman to woman-handle, if she has to.

Because there are so many women "into sheep", you might expect the Vanscoy Sheep Show to be quite crafty, and it is; there are producers spinning and weaving and knitting their own sheep's wool right on the spot.

I tasted barbecued lamb for the first time in my life and I am happy to say it was really good, because to say it was not would strain relations, I'm afraid, when I run into some sheep producers on my way home from the post office. Unfortunately, Vanscoy lamb costs more in the supermarket than New Zealand lamb does. Maybe the ships delivering it get some kind of a Crow rate; I don't see, otherwise, how they can possibly do it.

I got along very well with those local sheep at the Vanscoy Sheep Show when I walked the pens to talk to them. And it's to be a matter of record here that most of them said Ma-a-a! Ma-a-a! to me, most gently; they know a grey-haired mammy when they see one; only the very cynical said so much as one tiny Bah!

Hard on the heels of the Vanscoy Sheep Show I went off to the mountains to hike some nature trails in some glorious national parks. And there I met some more sheep and got goose-bumped down to my very toes like a little kid with the thrill of seeing seventeen scruffy mountain sheep cross the blacktop ahead of the car as though they owned both blacktop and car (and might repossess both at a moment's notice).

Of course they have a right to.

They own that land out there whether the human creature has wandered across it laying macadam all over it or not; and they own the human creature, too (or at least, they own his heart, unless that human creature came into this world without one).

Ninety-nine and forty-four one-hundredths per cent of us didn't though, so the mountain sheep and the mule deer and the black bear and the golden-mantled ground squirrel in Canada's national parks own us, through the heart, completely.

And what do ordinary, amiable, warm-blooded, nature-loving North Americans do for the creatures they love?

They feed 'em.

People are funny that way. When they love somebody, they feed them. Kids, dogs, neighbours, rabbits, hockey teams, cats, grandchildren: if we love them, we feed them. Whether they belong to us or not, we feed them.

And lots of time we feed them junk: potato chips, pretzels, sugar candy, pop. They're crazy about junk food and we love them and we have the money to buy the stuff, and we think we have the right to spoil all the lovely things we love because they want the things that we can give them. And so we feed them and pat them on the head while they're stowing it away; and we're happy because we have made them happy; and they're happy because they have all that yummy salt and sugar going down inside the tummy.

Well, I'm no kid anymore; and nobody feeds me anymore, I feed myself. But with me, hiking in the mountains, it was pretzels. I claimed it was because I was losing too much salt toiling like an old sick mountain sheep up and down those mountain trails. But it wasn't that; I'm just crazy about pretzels. I had some in my pocket all the time.

I did not offer them to mountain sheep or golden-mantled ground squirrels, because the two young people I was with would not allow it.

"Mother," said one of them, "if *I* had to eat all those green beans and all that spinach at your table when I was a kid so that

I wouldn't grow up looking tacky and scruffy, then the same goes for mountain sheep: they'd better stick to green beans and spinach, too. You'd just help to make bums of them by feeding them salted junk. Look at them already: scruffy; sad-eyed; salt sores all over their mouths . . ."

It was the salt sores that did it. I put the pretzels back in my back pants pocket.

But I got out of the car. The three of us did.

And the seventeen scruffy sheep came around to sniff us.

But I was the only one who had salted pockets. So they all crowded around me.

Close.

So close they started backing me up a mountain.

Seventeen sheep, all of them with salt sores!

So I started climbing the mountain.

And so did the sheep, who were much better climbers.

Faster and faster; higher and higher: a little puffing grey-haired Saskatchewan mama hounded over B.C. rock and stunted pine by seventeen sore-mouthed sheep.

"Way to go, Bo Peep!" From down below called the one who said I had her eat too much spinach and not enough junk food when she was a kid at my table. It took her and the health nut she's married to twenty minutes to believe I wasn't having a pile of fun up there on that rock with seventeen mountain sheep, all of them trying to climb into my back pants pocket. As soon as they rescued me I ditched those salty pretzels in the nearest garbage can.

We hiked for five more days and I didn't die for lack of salt even once.

When I got back home to Vanscoy, sound of wind and limb and mouth, I had half a mind to throw away the salt cellar forever.

FOWL SUPPERS, AND THINGS LIKE THAT

When you live in a little town, and help to make your living in a way that most people don't, you might wonder sometimes if people are soon going to start calling you "that crazy woman", but somehow, people just aren't made like that, here in Vanscoy.

Mostly they just seem to pretend I don't do crazy things like talking on the radio, or running around to read the stories and poems I write to folks in other little towns where the people don't have anything better to do than to come down to the library or the town hall and sit down for a whole hour and listen to stuff like that and in the middle of the day, too, sometimes.

But now and again, somebody will stop me when I am on the way to the post office in the morning and say, "Say, I heard you on the radio the other day talking about fowl suppers and that reminds me, you're on my phoning list so what can you bring, buns or pie or mashed potatoes for thirty, to this year's fowl supper?"

Everybody around here calls them fowl suppers. But when I was a kid we called them turkey suppers, or chicken suppers, or even fried rooster suppers. We weren't all that good on English vocabulary, most of us, in those days, except for the ordinary words (and the dirty words), and so we wouldn't have called them fowl suppers even if we'd heard somebody else call them that — say when we went to Saskatoon where people said and did outlandish things anyway, things we'd never get away with.

We had a teacher once who told us *foul* meant dirty — as in *foul-mouth,* you see. She was the one who washed your mouth out with soap, or had one of the Big Girls in school do it for you if you were a foul-mouthed little girl, or had one of the Big Boys do it for you if you were a foul-mouthed little boy and might even kick the teacher a good one if she undertook the mechanics of washing.

But I just forgot there for a minute, didn't I? We're talking about fowl suppers here; or at least one of us has claimed to be. So I guess I'll just tell you the first real, traditional, prairie, roast turkey fowl supper I can remember vividly is one I went to in Aberdeen. Aberdeen, Saskatchewan. I went when I wasn't a kid any longer and hadn't had my mouth washed out for a long time. And I was there anonymously—which means there was nobody there to remind me they knew my father or My goodness, yes, I sure was the spittin' image of my mother.

It was the one short year of my life when I wasn't anybody's anything: anybody's daughter or girl friend or wife or mother. And so I went to this fowl supper in Aberdeen and for the first time in my life I ate three pieces of pie, after a good turkey dinner, and was not reprimanded for it by the cook or my conscience or my stomach, and so I remember it yet.

I remember the whole thing, really. I remember the supper, the eating part, was in the basement of the church (or *a* church), and it couldn't hold everybody who wanted to help demolish that turkey. Not at one time. And so the late-comers stood around or sat around or squatted around in the warm October sun outside and talked, arms folded as they stood— those who stood. They talked mostly about the crops; they were mostly men just off the field and with fresh haircuts and with white Sunday shirts on but no ties, because it wasn't Sunday, or because the one who generally made them wear one was already down in the church basement and had been down there all afternoon getting ready to dish up golden turkey and mashed potatoes and gravy so brown you'd think it was pork, and turnips and green peas and three kinds of pie per customer if the customer had stomach enough to handle it.

So there was this whole bunch of folks that day in Aberdeen, that golden and sun-warm October day in Aberdeen, and those folks looked as beautiful as Saskatchewan farmers always look when they are just a whisker away from the wind and the fields that have tanned them so brown there is nothing like a white

Sunday shirt open at the neck to make them look even better than the turkey, just out of the oven and on its way to the fall fowl supper.

After everyone had eaten there was some music, I think, and a few recitations and the like of that; it's funny that my memory should fail me for what happened after we all got done with that turkey, and if you have taken a class or two at the university in Psychology you'll likely nod a bit inside yourself at that because you know that likely means something, that tells you something about my undernourished psyche, right?

I am not the one to deny any university-trained mind anything, so don't expect me to try.

I don't know, but some university-trained mind riding a tractor on a Saskatchewan field near Manor or Melfort might well have reckoned why people in this part of the world are so strong on fowl suppers. I have it on good authority that long hours inside the cab of a tractor are just the thing for reckoning out the idiosyncrasies of one's own society: why the CBC will ladle us out philosophy and opinion only in three-minute chunks; why your mother-in-law has served fried cabbage for every Sunday supper for the past eighteen years; why the pastors nowadays wear turtleneck sweaters when they come to visit; why you can't tell a nun from a real woman anymore by the clothes – and, why some people offer (and a whole lot more go to eat at) fowl suppers.

I suppose we could link in the harvest syndrome – the gathering in off field and garden and chicken coop all that must be done before Jack Frost and Old Man Winter pull in again on icicled sleigh runners to spoil it all. Or the need of a people not too far removed from a pioneering past to gather together to give thanks for what has been garnered and which will keep them alive during another long – and sometimes devastating – winter.

But that really isn't it; not all of it, anyway. For Thanksgiving – thanks to the early Yankee-ization of our Canadian mores – is sitting bold on the calendar already to take care of that need once the fowl supper is out of the way, or has already been thanked and turkeyed and pumpkin pied into memory by the time the local fowl supper wafts the heady aroma of sage and onion to those waiting in the pale autumn sun for their turn at table.

Some will say it all comes down to nothing more than the fact that the church needs a new altar cloth now and again or that the curling rink needs better ice-making equipment. For fowl suppers, of course, tend to be fund-raisers for the home community.

But I'll personally bet a purty that people don't go to fowl suppers to help buy the church a new altar cloth; we go, nowadays, because once we were children.

Once we were children who never questioned that our mothers would feed us adequately: porridge, perogies, bean soup, haggis, milk, and cornstarch pudding. We would always have enough to eat, or nearly enough, in one way or another. We also never questioned that an extra slice of pie—on those rare days when there *was* pie—was pie-in-the-sky optimism at our mother's kitchen table.

It was the same with chicken. You might have chicken every Sunday, especially if your dad had discovered chickens would grow when wheat wouldn't—all they needed was wheat screenings from the elevator, some oyster shell (to make sure the egg would come out of the chicken with a house around it rather than as wobbly wish-washy amnion), and a whole lot of grass-hoppers.

(I know, I know: Yukk! is right!) But even if you had chicken every Sunday you never ever had quite enough, especially if you lived too close to the church and so were pretty well guaranteed there'd be company for supper always to help lift everything but the pope's nose off the platter before it got to you at the kids' end of the long narrow table.

But a fowl supper was something else again. For one thing, you paid money for a fowl supper and so you were expected to eat your money's worth: your mother expected it and the providers of the supper did, too.

Another turkey drumstick? You bet. Good boy, you know how to eat, you'll make your daddy a dandy hired man if you just keep it up, let's feel that muscle. Another piece of pie? Surest thing in the world, sweetheart; do you want Gramma

Vandercoy's Dutch apple or Auntie Flo's lemon chiffon? Eat, eat, eat; it cost Papa fifty cents to bring you.

Eat, eat, eat. Show everybody how good it is, don't let the ladies suppose it didn't taste good enough to bring you back next year.

For that was another thing: appreciation. When someone does something for you, appreciate, darn it! It's tough enough living in hard times; be a dog in the manger when someone does something nice for you and you'll be a mighty lonely dog by the time you're pensioned off and finally have the time and the inclination to learn to appreciate.

Appreciate, at a fowl supper, the warmth of the serving hall and the warmth of the reception; the talk and the laughter and the music that followed the washing up; the turkey done to a turn and the apple pie sliced so generously it was sometimes almost impossible to consider a second helping.

Nowadays, I don't care for turkey, or even for pie, the way I used to. So I mostly go to wash dishes when there is a supper of any kind on at the Vanscoy Circle Hall. The people come from Saskatoon and for miles around, for the Vanscoy fowl supper. They are still lined up for the equivalent of a city block, as a rule, when I walk down with my apron on and ready to tackle the plates of those who've already had their innings with the turkey. The people stand very orderly and patiently—a thing that the British like to say the Germans do very well, though surely all those people who come to eat those Vanscoy-cooked turkeys can't all be Germans. They don't seem to talk much.

And hardly a one wears a white Sunday shirt open at the neck with no tie on, here in modern day Vanscoy, or Weyburn, or Montreal Lake, or in every other small Western town where there is bound to be a Railway Avenue, a Chinese cafe, a fall fowl supper, and a sawed-off Main Street.

THE NEW NON-ENGLISH

There used to be a time when words meant what they said; and so people, if they tried hard enough and were honest hard enough, meant what they said, too.

Not any more.

Or else, in the days when the Bible and William Shakespeare and the radio and newspaper and I all spoke the same English, I was so mesmerized by the melody and feeling of the language I just didn't keep my ears open.

Come to think of it, people often did used to tell me, at school, to get the wax out of my ears. But I knew they meant I better pay better attention, as for example on the ball diamond, where I'd tried to steal a base again when the whole team was hollering "Stay! Stay!" and so we'd lost another inning.

So maybe I never really learned English; maybe I just thought I did.

All the same, it sure seemed to me, that for the first forty-seven years of my life, Tom the Jersey bull was the only one I ever knew of who "serviced" anybody.

Or anything.

Because cars weren't even "serviced" then; they were fixed, or repaired, or had their oil changed or their spark plugs cleaned or their gas tanks filled.

Nothing and nobody got "serviced" except cows and new-blooming heifers.

Today, everything and everybody gets serviced.

Are you needing a healthy, new-blooming body? Are you needing a new car, a new cord for your toaster, a better perspective, a new Jersey bull? Why, COME RIGHT IN AND

LET US SERVICE YOU . . . the sooner the better, the oftener the better. So long as you've got the fee for the service.

(Tom used to get an extra measure of chop, as I remember.)

My father, who owned Tom, if a bull may be said to be owned by anybody but himself, indirectly *provided* a service, I suppose. But if he'd advertised in the *Farm and Ranch Review* that he stood ready to service all comers, he'd have taken such a razzing the next time he went to town that he, a stuffily moral man, wouldn't have dared to show his face ever again at the pool hall or the Wheat Pool elevator.

It's the same thing with "visitation". I'd swear that even a very few years ago the only people to make visitations were angels and ghosts and the Virgin Mary the time she went, according to St. Luke, to visit a needy Elizabeth.

Nowadays, if you go to visit your Uncle Luke in Virden, Manitoba for two days, it's called a visitation and gets written up as such in the local news in the paper.

I don't know why, but the "modern English usage" that bugs me the most used to be "that bugs me". But after over twenty years of being bugged by "that bugs me" I've finally come to accept it as not only apt and colourful for a society only one generation removed from the bed bug and army worm and grasshopper, but as a mere fly in the ointment compared to "Have a *fun* day, folks!"

A *fun* day (and a *fun* time, and a *fun* person—and a *fun* son, for Pete's sake) is/are a full can of unfunny worms so mishmashed no amount of Rawleigh's For Man or Beast salve could make them whole again.

I suppose that's because I was reared under the Holy British Imperial Empire School System that ruled Saskatchewan's young with an iron hand softened not one whit by the fact no one had dared to remove the portrait of the aged and dour Victoria from the front wall above the teacher's desk, though King Edward (the seventh one, not the one who gave up a crown for Wallis) and even a sixth George had a right by then to the central position.

What I call the Holy British Imperial Empire Saskatchewan School System did a heck of a lot more for the British Empire, as far as I can see, than it ever did for Saskatchewanians. We learned to be loyal British Empire subjects, proud as punch that the sun never set on the British Empire. But there's one thing it did do for us. We sure as shootin learned you did not say "sure as shootin" (or "ain't" or "I and him") in polite company; you did not (indeed, you dared not) play Norwegian singing games in the schoolyard (and under pain of death, German ones).

And you never, never, NEVER, did you hear me, class, never use a noun as an adjective; it just isn't done and that is that.

You use a noun as a noun — the name of a person, place, or thing. And *fun* is a noun: it is a some*thing*. You use an adjective as an adjective — to describe a person, place, or thing. And *fun* is not an adjective, it is a noun, remember? So you ought not to use it to describe a person, place or thing.

You can *have* fun *poking* fun at aging Saskatchewanians who are fusty-minded enough to crawl up the wall when you announce you "had such a *fun* time at an *old-fashion* fowl supper" the other night. Nonetheless, you are helping to maim what has been one of the most efficient (if not the most beautiful) languages to have evolved from human mind when you do so.

I won't even grit my teeth when you say "old-fashion" instead of "old-fashioned". I couldn't care less that people are dropping the ed's off words, for I'm too busy caring a whole lot that people can not recognize when they are speaking non-English. For, when someone says, "I could care less", most often what he/she means is exactly the opposite: I care so little that it is downright impossible for me to care one iota less.

Look at it this way: If it is your intention to indicate your *un*-caringness, why stipulate you have enough caring left in you to care a jot or a tittle *less?*

It pains me to continue. But how do you feel about a war being "down-sized" by Yankeeland sending a fleet of cruisers into a troubled part of the world in order to scare the combatants into de-fusing the issues? Are you happy to be "dialoguing" with your kids when their beds resemble rats' nests for the third day in a row? And do you intend to go out to the mall today to "shop

Safeway" while we tired old Rule Britannia grammarians are shopping *at* the IGA?

Let us not even consider going beyond the bounds of grammar and into the doubtful, manipulative psychology of "Have a good day". There was a time when "have a good day" meant you were being wished a good day. Now it automatically pours from the mouth of hardware store clerks and bureaucratic pen pushers who haven't provided what you came to them for and who could care less if you have a good day or a bad one, a fun day or one filled with troubles needing down-sizing.

I mean, we're talking disintegration of a language here, people; we're talking non-communication; we're talking obfuscation, fogginess: we're talking *about* the dangers of changing a once-useful tool, language, into an outpouring of sound that almost — but not quite — makes sense.

I wouldn't be a Taiwanese immigrant in this country for any amount of money nowadays, let me tell you.

I suppose, when all is said and done, it doesn't really matter. We live in an era of change, a time of challenge.

It's just I get so tired sometimes. To keep up with the times is hard enough when there's so much to keep up with. To get the wax out of your ears every time a word changes its meaning, though, is challenge too much, some days, for the likes of me, hanging on to the old ways, and an old house, here in a little Saskatchewan village, at the north end of Main Street.

REMEMBERING

There have been wars and rumours of war ever since the day in my life when I lost my innocence by hearing on my father's old battery Marconi radio that England, and therefore Canada, had gone to war against the Hun. So for me "The War" is World War II and not the Vietnam War or the Korean War or any other war that has raged and ravaged before or since.

Sooner or later wars have to end.

I don't remember very much about when the boys came marching home, or about when the girls came marching home — because of course they did, too; there just weren't any songs written about them; it somehow wasn't romantic enough for people to want to write and to sing about.

I guess I was too young to remember too much. I sometimes feel like the oldest woman alive on the face of the earth, but I suppose I am not, for I seem to have been too young to remember much about that war, or else I was too busy. By then we were living in town, a small town not much bigger than the town where I live now, and I was going around to people's houses, when they asked me to, to scrub and wax their kitchen floors for twenty-five cents, and so maybe I had my nose and eyes and ears too close to the squares or polka dots on somebody's kitchen linoleum and so I missed a lot of things.

I knew the war was over, though, when our soldier uncle and our airman uncle both showed up at my mother's house. They were her brothers. And they didn't come marching in at all; they came in looking tired and very, very sad.

Especially the airman uncle. He had been in the bombers. The bombers that flew over his father's fatherland. And when he came home again he stayed with us for a while; he couldn't trust himself to go home to his father's farm yet.

And he couldn't sleep. He walked the floor and walked the floor, the night had such terrors for him; the pictures of the bombings were still too alive on the moving picture screen inside his mind. My mother told me all this, because I asked her. That's the way she was. She protected us from too much else; she had to tell the truth about something so important.

Coming home was worse than dying, for some people. For those raw-nerved souls who could not bear pain, and so could not bear to inflict it upon others.

I am the same way myself, I think. Although I am, by name, a fighting spear maiden, I try to glide through life with my spear securely sheathed, and all my armour intact against incidental or accidental spears of others. My whole life now is a deliberate pretense that there is no deliberate pain in this world; some days that is the only way that I can function.

We are missing the boat somewhere, it seems to me, when we cause pain to others, no matter how it is done. But it is particularly black-souled when we do it with war, and give all sorts of excuses for it.

There have been other wars since the war that sent German Saskatchewanians onto German soil to kill and maim their cousins. There have been Hitlers to out-Hitler Hitler in other wars, but the war people seem to want to use to prove there should be no more wars is *that War*, not the war that killed more people in just as inhuman a way but is not used as a moral example by those who would teach us better. And I somehow hesitate to say the Korean and Vietnamese Wars are not used as an example because the people who were murdered had non-Caucasian genes.

I don't think I carried the guilt of Hitler on my shoulders, but maybe I don't know all I think I know about the little people-pleaser who hides inside the manufactured self. I know I have never ever felt very German. My mother would never permit it. To be German in any country but Germany led only to pain, she had already discovered. And she wanted to spare us that.

Besides that, the vibrant, efficient, British imperial school system made staunch British loyalists of us all, before we got out of grade four. Which seems to me to have been a pretty lucky thing for the British Empire, seeing a lot of us never made it to grade five.

From our German Saskatchewan farms our uncles and brothers and aunties and cousins went off to fight King George's war just as bravely and just as scared and just as devil-may-care as others did from all parts of that foolish Empire.

We were all of us foolish together, and I wish people would quit quoting me that second German war.

Most of the German Saskatchewanians I know today have come here from that old land since that old war which is being kept fresh year after year and decade after decade just by trotting out that same old name: Hitler. Other madmen are allowed to die, their mania and their sins not resurrected almost daily to prove we have learned so little since then that we have had Korea and we have had Vietnam.

I am tired of Hitler. I want to talk about the good and decent Germans I know who have come to a good land to make a good life and who want to forget pain for at least a little while, now and again, too. I have met these people, some of them, at Volkslieder Chor where I have gone this winter to learn the songs of my mother's people, and to try to become at least a little German, to match my genes, so that I can be whole.

These new Germans are generous of mind and heart and they are sharing of their energy and material goods. They do not call themselves Germans. They do not call themselves German Saskatchewanians, as I call them. They call themselves, always, German-*Canadians,* and when you meet them they never fail to say they are both proud and grateful to have been permitted to live in this land.

Saskatchewan is *my* home and native land, but I forgive them for choosing to put Canada first.

And there isn't a whole lot of time to bother about such things anyway, when you are Valleri-ing in the soprano section when you really belong with the altos. I tell you, you have got all you can do to just remember to keep the melody; you do not have time to give to any painful remembering.

QUEST FOR FEAR OF FIRE

I've always been scared spitless of fire, and I have always sort of wondered why. For the first twenty years of my life, it didn't matter too much because my mother always kept the home fires burning in the kitchen cook-stove and later on in the coal and wood furnace when we moved into town into an old two-storey house that seemed a palace compared to what we'd been living in on the farm.

When I was forced to face the realities of life, by agreeing to go and live in one little country teacherage after another, once the wood fire was lit in the morning by Joe Story, while I huddled under the feather tick, keeping it going was my job. Let me tell you, for the first two years, I never let it go out, once lit. Winter or summer, I stoked the wood and coal to it because I was afraid to light it again if it should go out.

By then I'd seen Joe Story merrily douse green poplar with coal oil to bring it to a blaze. Well, to tell the truth, he wasn't too merry about it. If it is hovering at thirty-two degrees in good old Fahrenheit in your own family kitchen and you're trying to beat the water in the water pails from freezing because the water in the tea kettle has already frozen, and you're in your bare feet on the kitchen linoleum which is so frigid it is curling up at the edges, why, you are not as merry as you might be, trying to light a fire out of green poplar wood.

But, as I say, in two years time I saw Joe Story light the morning fire in some pretty unorthodox ways, and I'd seen *his* father feed cut up rubber tires to a campfire blaze when we went fishing, as an experiment in using up old tires and in saving the trees from being used as firewood. (Don't bother; all you get is smoke and stink and very little heat.) So gradually I began to light fires whenever I had to in the kitchen stove and out at a fishing or trapping camp, but I spent so much time building walls of earth and stone to contain any outdoor blaze that I became known as "the builder", and people were always asking me if I meant to try a bridge next so the men wouldn't have to use the boat to go over to Pickerel Point to fish.

When we moved to this big old house here on the northernmost tail-end of Vanscoy I could have cried for pleasure when I found it had an electric cook-stove and a natural gas furnace. But Joe Story said "Phmph" and went to a farm auction sale and came home with an old wood heater with isinglass doors for which he had paid fifty cents and which he promptly installed in my town house kitchen, in case the power ever failed.

That very first winter we had a three-day snow and ice and blow, and since a gas furnace can't cut in if there is no electric switcheroo telling it to, we kept this house warm enough to live in by heaving the logs to that little old farm auction heater.

Now and again I used to speculate it might be nice to just light a fire in it, some winter evening, or some cool rainy summer evening, and just sit in front of it with the lights out as some people did in front of their beautiful fireplaces.

But somehow, in those busy, busy years when I was doing things and never stopping to listen to my mind for what I *ought* to do, it was quicker to just turn up the heat and keep the lights on and do some more chores so that there wouldn't be as many to do tomorrow.

It wasn't until I was living alone in this house and asking for ghosts to visit me that I began to sit, now and again, in front of that isinglassed heater, and listen to my mind watch the flames of the life-giving fire.

I never learned so much about anything in all my life as I did that first winter, because I learned all about myself and, as if that wasn't enough, I learned a heck of a lot about The Lord of the Order of All Things, while I was at it.

It happened—or at least a lot of it happened—in motion picture scenarios just behind the eyes.

I found out why I was afraid of fire.

It seems it had to do with the time, when I was about eight

years old, and it was summer, and getting on dusk, and my mother was hoeing turnips in the garden; and my sister was curling her hair with the hot tongs; and the hot tongs had to be heated for the curling over the flame of a coal oil lamp; and too near the coal oil lamp on her dresser hung a celluloid cupie doll from the Fair in Saskatoon.

And the cupie doll's celluloid and feathers caught fire, it was a fragile thing, as my sister was; and so did the bedroom curtains.

And I, who'd been watching quietly, for once, in hopes she'd curl my hair next, did not offer to help her or to save her but ran out the door instead, hollering "Fire! Fire!" to the four winds and to my mother in the garden. And my mother went right on hoeing turnips, as she said later, because I was forever crying Wolf anyway, and a "Fire! Fire!" from her youngest daughter was just so much patter from a travelling girdle salesman, and therefore to be ignored.

By the time our father, asleep in the next room with a broken leg and its fresh plaster cast, had awakened and hobbled in with his bed quilt to slap out the flames, I suppose my horror of fire was so entrenched I couldn't watch the flare of a match with equanimity.

So my mind said.

Some of the things my mind told me were not as easy to accept. Some of the ghosts who shared the flame were not as easy to accept. And when you live by yourself with only your mind and your sometimes-not-so-holy spirit for company, there are times when the only safety lies in a cozy warm kitchen with a tea kettle singing softly on the stove as your mother's tea kettle used to sing when you were very young and very safe because you didn't know too much and somebody else was in charge of keeping you warm.

But who can afford to keep a tea kettle singing on even a low back burner at the current price of The People of Saskatchewan's electrical power?

So it got so I would light the kitchen heater, late at night when my mind told me to, and put out the lights, and sit there in the old rocker a buddy of my dad's gave me when I first went to live in little country school teacherages a lot of years ago. And I would sit and rock and look into the flames and listen to what they told my mind about fire and people and wanting to *be* safe – and *feel* safe.

And that's how my mind trapped me into going to see the first movie I'd seen at a movie house in at least seven years.

It was called "Quest for Fire", and I went, as bid, even though it was one heck of a cold, raw, wind-snappy day and I had to stand outside the movie house for an hour in a line-up and nearly succumbed, though wearing my long winter underwear, the old-fashioned, plum, fleece-lined kind and not the newfangled thermal.

And once I got inside, and soaked up enough natural gas heat, paid for by the movie house management, to watch the screen and to flip the switch to put the Mind Speaker into gear, it was all, all, all, like the flames in my old heater had already told me: *He who has fire, has life.*

Fire makes you a god, if you have the Mind to use it.

It makes you safe.

It keeps you warm.

It makes the tea kettle sing,

oh sing;

it makes the tea kettle sing.

And it tends to make poets of those who once lived in little country teacherages with a man who got up, mornings, to light the first warming fire.

Poets sing sad sometimes. They are truth tellers and so they cannot help it.

But they are still singers, who have always to sing.

It is a painful obsession – albeit often a glorious one…to carry inside yourself a full-of-fire singer.

If you are upon a quest of sorts just now, it is almost in me to pray you do not come upon such a singer.

CHRISTMASES THAT WON'T STAY PAST

I never talk much about Christmas, and I don't really know why. When others begin to talk about Christmas in November (or the day after Christmas if they are children and have only just finished one but are already wondering when they can have the next) I am somehow silent and do not talk about Christmas myself.

I have written about Christmas a lot, though. I have written about Christmas back home on the farm so many times and in so many different ways that I can hardly remember the parts that really happened.

It's like this. When you are a writer and you are writing stories and poems, even if they are stories and poems about Saskatchewan, and even if they are about people that sound an awful lot like your own neighbours, there is no law that says those stories and poems have had to actually happen to you.

When I write stories, I lie, in a way. For the story might say, right there on the printed page before your eyes, "*I* went out to the barn and *I* saw the hired man kissing *my* sister." But it is all a lie. So the reader who whips back to the cover page to check the name of the writer of the book and then says, "Oh my goodness, this Gertrude Story went out to the barn and saw the hired man kissing her sister!" is not right. It is all a lie, so far as I and any hired man I ever knew and so far as my two sisters are concerned. When we lived on the farm my sisters were too young and too pure to get kissed by hired men and anyway, any hired man we ever had seemed to be a whole lot more interested in apple pie and whiskey and playing Black Jack than in kissing anybody, even babies who were always cute in those days and who seemed to never mind the tobacco smoke that hung around most hired men.

(I have not forgotten this is to be a piece about Christmas. It's just that I have to work my way up to things. It's my way, just as the hired men's way was to avoid kissing, back in the 1930's.)

To tell lies in your short stories used to be called Literary Licence. It was important. It was something to teach in the schools and university, so they put capital letters on it to make sure you listened. It meant that the writer was allowed to change things that really happened if the changing made the story better (or if it helped the writer not to get sued for having written it.) And I have now changed so many things, especially the Christmases that lie forty years and more in the past, that I can hardly remember which way is right anymore.

I am pretty sure I can remember though, the awfullest Christmas I had as a child. The awfullest school Christmas. It wasn't awful because I forgot my part for the Santa Claus play, or because I suddenly wet myself half-way through the Parade of the Wooden Soldiers drill. German Saskatchewanians, as a rule, had better discipline than that, even at the age of six or seven, and most of them hardly ever forgot anything, especially the things they learned at recess out behind the barn or the coal shed.

No, this school Christmas concert was the awfullest because I was ten years old and I was expecting two presents from the tree, and I got them. I was expecting two presents and one would be from the Salvation Army or from some Ladies' Aid in Saskatoon who made it a habit in those Depression days to reclaim and rebuild used toys and then send them to children worse off than their own. I guess we were. The other present would be from the person who drew my name in the Christmas Present draw.

(Big surprise! Don't tell anybody whose name you drew, and don't ask anybody if they'd drawn *your* name. Rules are rules.)

In three days' time we knew not only who had drawn *our* names, but who had drawn everybody else's.

My name was drawn by my aunt. By my mother's baby sister who was only two years older than I was. At her house things were not as tough as they were most places in those tough times. My mother's little sister got to go to town any Saturday she wanted to and she always got spend-money when she went, at least twenty-five cents.

I was sure I would get from her a copy of *Anne of Green Gables,* no sweat. I made a point of mentioning, over and over in her hearing, how much I admired *Anne of Green Gables* and how the school copy was just about worn out. (I borrowed it nearly every week as soon as the road allowance grass turned green, and took it along out on the road, to help me herd the cows.)

On Christmas concert night I got from the Salvation Army or the Saskatoon church ladies the cuddly baby doll that had been hung by Teacher and the Big Girls at the very top of the tree, just under the tree top holy angel. It was pink and lifelike and cuddly, and somebody had hand-knit pink booties and bonnet for it in the seed stitch. It was very pretty and I hated it on sight and thanked Jesu over and over that I was too old to have to get given a cuddly pink baby doll off the school Christmas tree.

When Teacher handed it me, she pretended it was a special favour to me. It was hard to say thank you. I can see that baby face and that seed stitch bonnet to this day; I don't even have to close my eyes.

My mother's baby sister gave me a necklace with a snake's head at the end. I nearly cried. That very night, at home, my mother took the pliers and decapitated the snake for me and said, "There, *now* it's pretty, isn't it?"

What could I say? I hated snakes, headless or otherwise, and the necklet lay in its box until I managed to lose it.

Forty years later, when I had learned to admire snakes, for their beauty and for their honesty, I discovered I had been born in the Chinese Year of the Snake and was therefore, something of a charmed creature.

That put a whole new light on the matter.

For a long time I searched hopefully through old trunks and boxes, stored for long years at my mother's, in hopes of finding that poor headless truth-teller so that I could charm her head back into life.

Then one late evening, sitting before the fire aglow in the old isinglassed heater in my Vanscoy kitchen, my holy Mind began to form for me, before my eyes, a beautiful silver chain. And I sat up quick, saying, "Oh, oh, it's the silver cord getting ready to be loosed and if I see the golden bowl broken next, I am a goner, right here in this old rocking chair in this old kitchen!" And so I lost it. But since I didn't die there right on the spot, I relaxed again, and trusted again, and lo and behold, (as that other old storyteller said about another revelation), the chain formed again, its silver length divided into precise and lovely silver snaky scales. And then the head formed, with wise, wise eyes which looked me right in the eyeball and said, "There you are, sweetie; I'm whole again in the mind, and that is all that really matters, isn't it?"

I got up and went to bed and slept like a baby, and I dreamed about Christmas concerts in which young children sang carols as sweetly as angels, and Santa Claus, when he came, looked like my opa, the day before he died.

WINTER, 'WAY BACK THEN

I used to love winter, 'way back then, when I was a kid, and I really don't know why. We lived in a little four-room shack, a little slant-roofed shack, so we could go to a school that was close; and although the house on my father's home place was ever so much bigger and nicer, we never lived there again.

It got so cold in that little shack, when a snowstorm was howling, that my mother shut off the kitchen and the girls' bedroom, and we sat it out in the parlour (for nobody had front rooms or family rooms then) with my mother cooking us something hot on top of the Quebec heater, and managing somehow to keep us off each other's backs, and throats, for the storm's duration.

There were five of us then, and the one baby boy was still sleeping in a crib in our parents' room. The second boy got snuggled, those stormy days, between my two older sisters on the davenport, which was a settee by day and made into a bed for the night.

There was no room in the parlour for another bed, so my mother always made me one out of the davenport chair and two kitchen chairs and my father's arm chair. The davenport chair was the head and my father's chair was the foot, and the two kitchen chairs facing each other were the sides; so I was encased, as in a cocoon or a baby's crib, once she'd laid in a feather tick for a mattress and maybe three extra pillows for padding here and there. A lot of padding was needed, let me tell you, because the only place there was room for this odd bed was right against the draughty door that let to the small verandah.

I always felt kind of special because I got this bed. I'm sure now I got it simply because I was short enough to fit it and yet old enough not to get pneumonia sleeping in it, as our little brother might have done.

Also, it seems to me now, my two older sisters were rather political in those days and pretty good at lobbying our mother as to who would be shoved into that narrow davenport bed with them for as long as the storm lasted. They've never said, but I'm sure now they would much rather have had a cute, cuddly and biddable three-year-old than a strapping spear maiden of eight who kicked in her sleep and was not above laying a black eye to left or right whilst fighting dragons in her dreams.

However it happened, I got the makeshift bed, and I always felt special to get it.

One of the reasons I felt special, I suppose, is that my mother always got up, at least four times a night, to see if I'd kicked the covers off and was lying exposed to pneumonia and the draughty verandah door with nothing on but a flannelette nightgown, and a toque, and a pair of my father's wool socks, and sometimes even mitts if she'd been able to persuade me.

I always worried about her feet getting cold when she got up to check on me. And so I always called, very earnestly, "I'm OK, I'm OK," as soon as I awoke to her and the coal oil lamp advancing towards me. But she always came anyway, and made such a thorough inspection for bare skin, I'm sure her own feet didn't warm up again before it was time to do it all over again.

She was a very careful woman.

I was not a careful child. Outside, in the snow of winter, I would charge zappo on my sled down hills at night under a hard white winter moon, with utter disregard for rocks or barbed wire or for old machine parts lying just under the snow to whap me. My sisters were too old and kitchen-conditioned to join me and the little boys, thank goodness, were too young to go out at night although they begged.

My only companion was a series of dogs, all of them part collie and part camel, and with names I have forgotten. I do know they were always called names like Jiggs or Moon Mullins or Orphan Annie. My father had this way to name his animals after comic strip characters or movie stars. I bet we were the only people in Saskatchewan to own an ugly dirty black stallion called Silver, as soon as The Lone Ranger began to ride the airwaves.

But that's another story, and has nothing to do with winter. Which I loved, when I was a kid, back home on the farm with lots of things besides a care-full mother.

I wasn't much for making snowmen, as I remember. And they weren't too popular with any of my school chums, it seems to me. Snowmen were made by Dick and Jane in the school readers and by city kids in Saskatoon who had nothing more challenging than imitation in their heads — and a postage stamp-sized yard to imitate in.

On the farm we made igloos, Eskimo igloos, snitching our dads' long butcher knives for slicing the blocks out of hard-packed snowdrifts that reached half-way to the eaves of the granaries. We built fur trappers' forts, in the schoolyard, and yearned to steal the school's Union Jack to fly bravely above them.

One year a sister and I carved livingrooms and kitchens and bedrooms out of a great bank, sculpting a stove here, a bed or chair there (snow dishes were added later), so that our respective houses needed only the "loan" of horsehide robes to serve as roofs. We "visited" back and forth for three days, making each other snow tea in snow cups at fifteen below zero; then another storm hit and our houses disappeared under fresh hard drifts. I suppose we went on to other adventures then, but I remember those houses with a great deal of pleasure yet — and still relish making a place to live out of next to nothing.

Winter back then, it seems in retrospect, was a shining, shimmering, sun-lit, startlingly white world we lived in. There are days, now, when I might say if you have never seen kitchen window panes frosted over — on the *inside*, mind you — you haven't missed a heck of a lot. Those are the winter days when I have faced a bitter north wind bearing needle-edged snow on my way home with the mail, days when three vulnerable fingers have gone white by the time I am safe inside again.

But on the days when I do not have to brave the cold I stand at the large kitchen window that gives me such a gallant view of the countryside, summer and winter, and I remember the tiny kitchen window pane in the little lean-to shack on the prairie. You could often see nothing at all of the outside world for the glass was all frosted over. Oh, if you took the hot stove lid lifter and held it against the frost you could melt enough of a peephole to check if your dad was coming up the lane yet with a load of wood, but the peephole never lasted long, you can bet on it.

But why would you want to burn a dark hole, anyway, in the gloriously patterned white world that had grown on "Jack Frost's canvas"? (We had a teacher once who called winter farm windows that. We pretended to make fun of such airy-fairy notions but I, for one, in my secret heart-of-hearts, was more than willing to travel by way of the silver mind into the delicate tracery of the forested land that lived on my mother's kitchen window.)

My mother, I have always thought, was happier than I was when Joe Story bought me a big house with golden oak floors and with large windows guarded from frost through the joint miracles of a gas furnace and modern-day insulation. It was no fairyland to her, I know, and no picnic, either, living behind those Depression Days frosted windows.

For years we lived — Joe Story and the two children and I — in little old country teacherages and they sometimes also had winter fairylands traced on the kitchen windows. My mother tightened her mouth when she saw that and wished me better for the future.

Why is it now then, I wonder, that I so often become a child again, sitting cozily, nights, before the old wood heater I light when the sun goes down? There I sit and watch the fire's myriad suns dance behind the tiny isinglass "window panes" in the door of that handsome old heater. Why do I drift into the corners of the mind-that-is-always-silver to career downhill on my father's dirt farm to the shrill yapping of a yellow pup-collie?

And why, as I get older, do the fairyland patterns of frosted windows mean more to me — in the mind — than the real comforts of this solid and cozy house on the very edge of Main Street?

ROBERT "THE LADY BUG" BRUCE

When I was a kid and going to a little British Imperial Empire school in the wilds of Saskatchewan about twenty miles from Saskatoon in the unholy 1930's, I fell in love with the Scots and their wars and their quarrels and their bloodshed. And it was not until at least thirty years later that Mind told me there was not a heck of a lot of difference between the quarrelsomeness of the hillbilly Martins and McCoys (whom I did *not* admire) and those noble and brave and determined Scots. What difference there was had to do, Mind insisted, with poetry. The bards and historians who wrote the stories of the clansmen, to be devoured by avid hearts and minds in little Saskatchewan schools by the favour of his royal British majesty's school system, were holy singers all; they knew how to use language to capture the hearts and the sympathy and the loyalty of those who would but listen.

Once I knew the secret I went my own way and no longer cursed the Lutheran God who had let me be born non-Scots.

In the meantime, I traded that Lutheran God for a kinder power whose name, as delivered into my mind nights in dreams, over and over and over until I caught on and accepted, was The Lord of the Order of All Things.

If you started at the beginning of this book and worked your way so far, sometimes wondering what the deuce I was talking about, now it is a little bit clearer; am I right?

Then I am ready to report that I've been sharing my house this winter with an even quirkier individual. The Lord of the Order of All Things is bad enough, for he/she/it is fond of jokes and things that I am not much fond of, and so I have to learn to live with his/her/its quirkiness and learn to laugh at things I did not want, once, to laugh at.

Well now, this winter as another little joke, the order of all things delivered to my house this odd-ball to live with for a while.

I am not sure I should tell about it. I mean, unless you're struck on fables and morals and myths and legends, you'll likely think I've got a bit addled and quirky-minded myself, and belong in the booby hatch for safekeeping.

The thing is, I've been sharing my house with a lady bug who thinks she is Robert, "The Bruce"—or at very least, his spider.

Now, in case you yourself have not been indoctrinated by the Saskatchewan British Imperial school system, maybe I'd better say that Robert, "The Bruce", was Robert, the First, of Scotland (whenever the English let him be), and he defeated the English at the Battle of Bannockburn in 1314, so assuring the independence of Scotland and of oatmeal porridge and leaving all Scotsmen free forever to burn as much bannock as they choose.

He had his ups and downs, of course, did Robert, that Bruce. What dedicated and bloody-minded king in those days didn't? And during one of his "downs" he was hiding away in a cave, licking his wounds, so to speak, and wondering if he should take one more crack at saving Scotland for the Scots (and, incidentally, for the Bruces).

In the meantime, there was a spider in the same cave, also having a downer, for it was taking crack after crack at climbing a thirty-foot wall—or else making a thirty-foot Tarzan-style swing on a strand of his own rope, from one wall to the other; I forget which. In any case, he wasn't making it.

Anyway, Robert, "The Bruce", watched this for quite a while. And then he said to himself, out loud so he could be sure he meant it, "Ay'll bide by the wee crawler therre. Does he mayke it the next swing, ay'll take anither go at bashin' th' English, mysel', see if ay don't!"

And the spider did; and Robert, "The Bruce" did; and presto! The Battle of Bannockburn and independence.

Well then, this ladybug I'm living with in my Vanscoy cave this winter has got the same mentality. She keeps trying to climb the cold slidey picture-glass kitchen window, morning after morning, while I'm looking out at the world and eating my breakfast. She hasn't made it to the top in two hundred and thirty-seven tries, but she's still trying.

It got so I didn't know what to do about her anymore. I mean, it's very trying to be faced with such dedicated persistence at such an early hour every morning, even in dedicated and persistent Saskatchewan.

The other morning I decided to distract her to a higher purpose, because, well, I guess I didn't want any Bannockburns waged in my kitchen; I've burned enough stuff for one oven and seventeen kitchens in the thirty-seven years I have tried to become a cook. Anyway, this particular morning I was having jam tarts and ice cold milk for breakfast, a pleasure I never permitted my children when they lived under my roof, on the grounds that it was ruinous for the stomach.

And the lady bug fell off the picture-window, crash, right onto my breakfast tray, right smack onto her two black spots, and lay there panting. And, not even thinking, I droppped a crumb of gooey jam onto her madly moving mandibles. And she stopped panting and lay there saying "Mmmm!" instead.

Two hours later she was still at it. I checked her with a magnifying glass. She'd worked the jam tart crumb down to half-size by then and was practically comatose with pleasure.

The next morning she was sitting on the edge of my breakfast plate before I even had the coffee boiled. I was having plain old Scottish oatmeal. The pantry was right out of jam tarts.

I guess there was quite a bit of Bruce or MacLaren or Mac-Farland in her, all right, even though filtered somewhat by the plains of prairie Saskatchewan, because she seemed to gum down that porridge even more greedily than she had the jam tart.

We're just too sensible for words here, in the little prairie village of Vanscoy.

BEGINNINGS AND ENDS OF THINGS

When you come to the end of a book, The Writer Inside tells you, "That's enough, now," and so you know that you are done. She is a handy one to have around, this Writer Inside, for she knows where to start, and she knows what to say, and she knows when you should end.

It is a very comforting thing to have that Writer Inside inside you, for then you don't have to concern yourself about where the words will come from; you only have to concern yourself with making sure there are plenty of pens and that there is plenty of paper. Then you simply make the time to sit down and take the words down, the words The Writer Inside tells you, out of the right-hand side of your head, into the receiver on your left—and there it is; the writing is done; and there is silence up there in your head from where she does her talking.

But as soon as you say, "OK, then," and lay down the pen, there she is; she begins again.

"Nothing is ever done," she says, "it is only brought to an ending. And one ending is as good as another, for each is only a jumping off place, in order to start again."

"Start what?" say I (for of course you are free to talk to The Writer Inside, just as you are free to talk to God; in fact, The Writer Inside, I have found, is apt to talk to you a whale of a lot quicker and clearer than God ever did when He was in your head).

"Start anything," says The Writer Inside. "Start another book . . ."

"Never!" say I.

"Don't interrupt," says The Writer Inside, who tends to be a bit bossy when you do that. "Start anything you want: another book, another life, another season, another something that is something and has some pleasure attached."

There was silence again. So that seemed to be the end of that. But, as *I* wasn't quite done with that, but didn't know quite what to do about it, I just sat still for a while to see what else was getting in on the act.

I have learned that when The Writer Inside gives up on me, gives no more words to me, it sometimes means I have heard all there is to say, but it sometimes means only that I have run out of vim and vinegar and blood sugar (or at least the body machine has).

And so sometimes I trot to the pantry to see if there is something good there; and if there is nothing good I take something healthy; and if it is noon, it doesn't matter, I sometimes have porridge for lunch.

Then when the machine has been refuelled I let it all sit awhile. I look out the window and watch the juncoes and the sparrows feeding off Marigold and California Blue Eyes seeds in the bed I made overtop the old well.

It's April again, and snow still lingers between the one row of caraganas and the row of maples on the north side of the yard. And today there was morning cloud to gladden the hearts of the weather men who were paid yesterday to say it would rain today.

But my mind sat me down this morning, before turning me over to The Writer Inside, and denied those TV weather men. "Rain?" my mind said. "Why, my goodness, take a look to the northwest there, there lies your Dutchman's blue."

When I was a child, Richie and Bernice and Thelma, who lived on the farm across the road from our farm, and who knew all kinds of sayings I had never heard before and so made me jealous for their knowing them, used to say it would never rain so long as there was enough blue in the sky to make a Dutchman a pair of pants.

In the grade three reader there was the story of the little boy who saved Holland by sticking his thumb in a leaky dyke to hold back the raging sea. I used to be glad, on school Picnic day, sometimes, that he was not a very big Dutchman, for there was not a lot of blue sometimes, standing between a happy picnic day and one that was called on account of rain, and I always hoped that Lutheran God I used to pray to would take into account the picture of the boy in the grade three reader, kneeling at the dyke in his little Dutchman-blue pants, and not opt for a big, big Dutchman the size of Mr. Henrik Bakker who lived in Kilmeny district and whose daughter, if we were awfully lucky, might get to become our aunt.

That saying about a Dutchman's pants worked well, I know now, only because it was said in The Dirty Thirties, a time when the darkest sky most often gave no rain.

Now, that was another beginning there; the start of another story, the roots of another memory that has circled back to my computer-mind from its beginning somewhere in the past.

Living alone, you learn to look for connections like that. They ground you. They help you to be aware that they and you are a sure and secure part of the web-of-all-things, or the order-of-all-things, and so you are never really alone.

There are two robins, for instance, who have just hopped into my life as I write, sending the juncoes and sparrows scurrying to peck elsewhere. They are not only my gift for the day from the Lord of the Order of All Things, they are the end of a thought which will be the beginning of a poem or a memory that will begin, so:

The first two April robins
take over a territory
large enough for two
robins who need no
other
to complete the whole
circle of coming
     going
     returning
ever
to begin another
one.

Those who read between the lines of such things as poems

will read there more than a story about robins returning in spring.

And those who live alone in big old houses set on the edge of small towns, so they may look into the sunset — those who sometimes yearn to be where the sunset is — they will accept the hope (and the discipline) of another spring, another new beginning. And they will begin another day, and another day, secure in the knowledge of robins; secure in the knowledge of omens; secure in the knowledge that there is no real beginning of anything, and no real end of anything, just as there is never any end of new beginnings so long as the heart is true; the mind, sincere, secure.

369 23